INDIANA

Off the Beaten Path

W9-AKB-320

"Very handy for anyone 'wandering Indiana.' An excellent guide."
—Tim Walter, News Director, WOAV/WRTB Radio, Vincennes, IN

"The Thomases are residents of Indiana and know the back roads of the Hoosier state which lead to many special and unusual places. The guide also includes places to eat and stay and is divided into the five geographical areas."
—*The Star*, Chicago, IL

"Traveling by car doesn't mean you have to stick to the interstate highways. **Indiana: Off the Beaten Path** points out sights that most books miss."
—*News-Democrat*, Belleville, IN

"Well-organized, packed with information, and written with informal clarity. Whether you're just passing through a corner of the state or have lived in Indiana all your life, the book will tell you what's where in Indiana."
—*Palladium Item*, Richmond, IN

"A reference book to delight every age and interest group."
—*Tribune-Star*, Terre Haute, IN

INDIANA

Off the Beaten Path

Second Edition

by **Bill and Phyllis Thomas**

A Voyager Book

The Globe Pequot Press

Chester, Connecticut

The prices and rates listed in this guidebook were confirmed at press time. We recommend, however, that you call establishments before traveling to obtain current information.

Library of Congress Cataloging-in-Publication Data

Thomas, Bill, 1934-
    Indiana : off the beaten path / Bill and Phyllis Thomas. — 2nd ed.
      p.   cm.
    "A Voyager book."
    Includes index.
    ISBN 0-87106-669-6
    1. Indiana—Description and travel—1981- —Guide books.
I. Thomas, Phyllis, 1935- . II. Title.
F524.3.T47 1989   88-21432
917.72'0443—dc 19   CIP

Cover illustration by Kenn Compton.
Typesetting by The Repich Group, North Branford, CT

Manufactured in the United States of America
Second Edition/Second Printing

Indiana

Contents

Hall of Fame Museum, Indianapolis

Introduction

Ask almost anyone what images Indiana brings to mind, and—after a long pause—he's likely to mention the Indy 500, cornfields, and perhaps the steel mills of Gary. This book has been written to advise you that Indiana offers a lot more than racing, corn, and steel.

State highways and byways lead to some of the finest travel gems in the nation. There are natural wonders and manmade splendors, irreplaceable slices of Americana and futuristic marvels, places stately and sublime, others weird and wacky—a cornucopia of attractions, restaurants, and inns that for the most part lie off the well-trodden paths and are overlooked by major travel guides.

The most difficult part of writing this book was not deciding what to include, but what, because of space limitations, to leave out. Therefore, what you will find within these pages is merely a sampling of all that Indiana has to offer. It is our sincere hope that this book will help awaken your sense of adventure and encourage you to seek out other such places on your own.

Indiana's geography is sometimes a bit puzzling to strangers. They are often surprised to learn that South Bend is one of the northernmost cities in the state, while North Vernon is not far from the Ohio River, which forms Indiana's southern boundary. Along the Ohio-Indiana border on the east lies West College Corner, while way down in the southwest corner, just across the Wabash River from Illinois, there's East Mt. Carmel. And the towns of Center, Center Square, and Centerville are about as off-center as you can get.

To further confuse the traveler, a look at the official state road map (available free from the Indiana Department of Highways, Room 1106, State Office Building, 100 North Senate Avenue, Indianapolis 46204–2249; 317–232–5115) reveals four Buena Vistas, three Fairviews, three Georgetowns, three Jamestowns, two Klondykes and one Klondike, three Mechanicsburgs, four Millersburgs, five Mt. Pleasants, three Needmores, and four Salems. Pairs of towns with the same name are too numerous to mention, but would you believe *two* Pumpkin Centers? No wonder the U.S. Post Office insists upon zip codes!

But never mind—this book will at least put you in the right county. And if you do get lost, you're likely to meet such warm, friendly people along the way that you won't mind it a bit.

1

If all else fails, you can always call the twenty-four-hour toll-free Wander Indiana hotline for help. Dial 1–800–2–WANDER (292–6337). You may also write to the Indiana Department of Commerce, Tourism Development Division, One N. Capitol St., Suite 700, Indianapolis 46204–2288; 317–232–8860.

Happy wandering!

Off the Beaten Path in Central Indiana

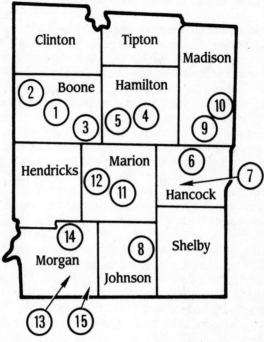

1. Boone County Courthouse/ Donaldson's Country Home Candy Shoppe
2. Garden of Memories
3. Zionsville Colonial Village
4. Conner Prairie Pioneer Settlement/Indiana Transportation Museum/ Canterbury Arabian Horse Farm
5. Camel Lot
6. C. C. Irving Wild Game Farm
7. Riley Memorial Park/Old Log Jail Museum
8. Johnson County Museum
9. Anderson University
10. Camp Chesterfield/Mounds State Park
11. Indianapolis Museum of Art/ Indianapolis Zoo/Garfield Park Conservatory
12. Indianapolis Motor Speedway/Hall of Fame Museum
13. Grassyfork Fisheries, Inc./ Midwest Phonograph Museum
14. Goethe Link Observatory/ Link Daffodil Gardens/Gravity Hill
15. Rock House Inn

Central Indiana

Boone County

The entire community has pitched in to help restore the glory of yesteryear to Zionsville's 125-year-old downtown business district, and its citizens have succeeded admirably. Now known as the **Zionsville Colonial Village,** it's filled with interesting shops to explore. Tiddlywinks' Toys carries teddy bears, wooden trains, and collectible dolls. At Calico Corners, you can purchase designer fabrics at a discount. Three buildings with vine-covered walls, filled with a variety of unusual items and nestled in a garden setting, are known collectively as Brown's Antiques.

In the heart of the village is Adam's Rib, often selected as one of the Indianapolis area's ten best restaurants. The adventurous come here to sample the appetizers—such exotic treats as buffalo hump, llama, giraffe, camel, alligator, zebra, antelope, gnu, lion, kangaroo, and rattlesnake. All of this unusual fare is not available at all times, so it's best to call ahead if you're yearning for something special. However, you can enjoy excellent American and continental cuisine any day except Sunday. The prime rib and fresh seafood have been luring customers back for years. Prices are moderate to expensive, and reservations are advisable for dinner. Located at 40 South Main Street, it's open 11:00 A.M. to 3:00 P.M. Monday through Saturday; 5:30 to 10:00 P.M. Monday through Thursday; 5:30 to 10:30 P.M. Friday and Saturday; (317) 873-3301.

For additional information, contact the Greater Zionsville Chamber of Commerce, P.O. Box 148, Zionsville, 46077; (317) 873-3836.

The **Boone County Courthouse** in Lebanon, built in the early 1900s, once drew sightseers from around the world. They came to marvel at the eight limestone columns that adorn the north and south entrances. Each gigantic pillar—38 feet high, 4 1/2 feet in diameter, weighing about forty tons—is shaped from a single block of limestone.

Lebanon is also the home of Indiana's answer to Willie Wonka's chocolate factory. Any chocoholic worth his salt will love a tour of **Donaldson's Country Home Candy Shoppe.** Watch through glass doors as chocolates are cooked in cooper kettles and fudge is kneaded on a marble slab. Guides are on hand to explain the history of this favorite flavor. Donaldson's

4

produces and sells nearly sixty kinds of candy, including almond bark, chocolate-covered caramels, hand-dipped creams and assorted nut clusters. Just when you think you can't stand it another minute, you're given a free sample. The tours won't cost you a cent, and you're certainly under no obligation to buy a thing, but if you don't, you have more will power than most of us. You'll find Donaldson's across from the Holiday Inn on State Road 39, just south of State Road 39's intersection with Interstate 65 on the south side of Lebanon. Stop by anytime between 9:00 A.M. and 6:00 P.M. Monday through Saturday but try to avoid November and December. They're understandably very busy months. The management would appreciate it if you could give them at least one day's advance notice for a guided tour; (317) 482–3334.

Approximately 5 miles north of Thorntown, along Highway 52, motorists can pause at a pretty roadside stop to eat a picnic lunch and enjoy the pleasant rural panorama. There all similarity to other roadside stops ends, for this is the home of the **Garden of Memories,** a spiritual refuge that is a true labor of love. Reverend Alan Moody, pastor of the nearby Walnut Grove Community Church, first saw the garden in a vision, and now the vision is well on its way to becoming reality. At present, the garden is surrounded by a stone wall that forms the outline of a king's crown. Each of the crown's six points is topped by a glass globe that's lighted all night during summer months and until late in the evening during winter. When you walk through the stone archway in the wall, you're confronted by a rock pile that supports three wooden crosses. There are also winding walkways, a baptismal well, a statue of Christ, and a tiny stone chapel. Eventually, Reverend Moody and his interdenominational congregation hope to build a church adjacent to the garden. At the entrance to the roadside rest area, a sign reads: "Garden of Memories—Welcome!" It is altogether a serene and lovely place to be. For additional information, call Reverend Moody at (317) 436–7166 or 436–7029.

Clinton County

People in Indiana will drive miles for a good catfish dinner—and when they do, chances are they'll be heading for Miller's Fish Suppers in Colfax. A fixture on the Colfax scene since it first opened its doors in October 1946, Miller's occupies an aqua concrete building at the intersection of Oakland and Railroad streets. The setting is pure Americana—a tiny town, population 800, presided over by a rickety water tower and surrounded by rural countryside. The only anachronism is the mass of humanity that invades Miller's Restaurant.

Most likely you'll have to take a number, then wander through the crowd outside and find a curb to sit on or a wall to lean against until your number is announced over the loudspeaker system. While you wait, sniff the aroma of catfish wafting through the air, make new friends among the other catfish addicts in line, watch the smiling faces of sated patrons as they waddle out to their cars, note the various makes of cars parked on nearby streets (Cadillacs, Lincolns, and Mercedes are usually mixed in among Fords, Chevrolets, and Volkswagens), and check license plates to see how many states are represented (you'll probably be surprised at just how far some people will come for superlative catfish).

When at last you're seated, you'll find that the menu does list other entrees—chicken, shrimp, steak—all of which are quite good. But as proprietors Meikel and Beckie Miller will tell you, the catfish is king. Approximately 85 percent of the meals served are catfish. Once you taste them, fresh from catfish ponds and deep-fried in their crunchy cornmeal coating, you'll understand why. Meikel (Mike for short) estimates that he fries approximately 3,000 pounds of catfish a week. Did Mike get into this business because he loves catfish himself? No, he never touches the stuff—turns out he's allergic to fish.

Accompanying the star attraction—three whole catfish per dinner—are French fries, a salad (the homemade cole slaw with sweet and sour dressing is recommended), bread right off the shelves of the grocery store, and coffee. But do yourself a favor and order the fried onion rings. If people didn't like Miller's catfish so much, they'd probably come anyway for the onion rings. And maybe for the strawberry shortcake.

Prices are inexpensive to moderate, and the servings are generally humongous. Miller's is open from 4:00 to 10:00 P.M. Tuesday through Saturday; (317) 342–2656.

Hamilton County

Bed-and-breakfast accommodations are springing up all across the country these days, and many offer distinctive features, but there's probably only one where you can breakfast with two Siberian tigers. Besides welcoming overnight guests, owner Moselle Schaffer breeds exotic animals on a forty-eight-acre farm named **Camel Lot** near Westfield. The farm is not open to the general public because the insurance costs would be horrendous, but overnighters are welcome to roam the farm at will. Unfortunately, the camels that inspired the farm's name are no longer here, but there are llamas, zebras, deer, and tigers.

Guests stay in a private wing of the gray stone house, which contains a three-room suite complete with four-poster bed, private bath, air-condtioning, and a sitting room in which a camellia tree grows through the ceiling. A full breakfast is served, and if you choose, you can enjoy it on a terrace overlooking the pens of the farm's two resident tigers, Boris and Roberta Natasha.

Since Ms. Schaffer opened her bed-and-breakfast operation, she has been constantly surprised at its popularity. Her guests have come from all over the world, but her very first customers lived a mile down the road. The second customer stayed three months.

Rates are $60 a night for two. Contact Camel Lot, Ltd., 4512 West 131 Street, Westfield 46074; (317) 873–4370. Westfield is located just west of Noblesville, via State Road 32.

At **Conner Prairie Pioneer Settlement,** ranked as one of the nation's top five "living museums," it will remain 1836 forever. A restored pioneer village breathes life into history, permitting visitors to wander at their leisure through the homes, shops, school, and other buildings that might have made up a pioneer community. "Residents" keep busy at tasks that must be performed to keep the settlement going, while at the same time answering questions about their life-style.

Meticulous research, constantly ongoing, helps assure the authenticity. The orchard, for instance, was first planted in neat rows, but when it was learned that this was a twentieth-century method, fruit trees were scattered about at random. It was also discovered, much to everyone's surprise, that men did not wear beards in 1836, and all whiskers except mutton chops had to go. All lace trim had to be removed from the women's dresses—that was a no-no, too.

Also located on the 250-acre tract is a Federal-style mansion built in 1823 by Indiana statesman William Conner. Visitors can tour the main house and grounds, which feature a spring house, a still, and a loom house where Conner Prairie staff members duplicate textiles used during the 1830s.

Conner Prairie Pioneer Settlement

At the Prairie Adventure Center, trained craftsmen are on hand to assist visitors who want to learn pioneer skills firsthand. You can try your hand at such pastimes as weaving on an authentic loom, making candles, and whittling with period tools.

The Museum Center includes a shop that sells items hand-crafted by Conner Prairie artisans, a restaurant that features a mix of modern and historic foods, and a bakery that offers nineteenth-century breads, pastries, and cookies.

Special events are also in keeping with the times. Once a month, the Methodist circuit rider arrives to preach his sermon. A presidential election is held in the fall, just as it was in 1836. Weddings, too, are authentic, and it often comes as a surprise to visitors to learn that even in the mid-1800s women did not promise to "obey" their spouses. Brides agreed to "love, honor, and assist" their husbands, who in turn promised to "love, honor, and maintain" their wives.

A program of Earlham College in Richmond, Conner Prairie is located 4 miles south of Noblesville. Open 10:00 A.M. to 5:00 P.M. Wednesday through Saturday and noon to 5:00 P.M. Sunday, early May to late November; also open 10:00 A.M. to 5:00 P.M. Tuesday, May through October and at other times for special events; closed Easter and Thanksgiving. Admission is charged. Write Conner Prairie Pioneer Settlement, 13400 Allisonville Road, Noblesville 46060; (317) 776-6000.

At the **Indiana Transportation Museum** in Noblesville, you can follow the development of transportation in America, beginning with covered wagons. There are buggies, automobiles, trucks, fire engines, and trains to sit in and climb onto, and a clanging trolley to ride along a 1-mile track. The museum is in Forest Park, just north of Noblesville on State Road 19. It's open noon to 5:00 P.M. Saturday, Sunday, and holidays, mid-March to mid-November; nominal admission fee; (317) 773-6000.

The **Canterbury Arabian Horse Farm,** also north of Noblesville, welcomes visitors, free of charge, most any time. You can pet a horse's nose, see a horse "take a shower" in a wash rack, look on as the animals are exercised, stroll through a state-of-the-art barn that rivals horsedom's finest, and if your timing is right, watch a foal being born. Owners Flois and Debbie Burrow, who acquired their first Arabian in 1980, currently own twenty horses and board twenty more. To substantiate their claim that they have some of the best Arabians in the country, they point out two bulletin boards covered with show ribbons. The Burrows' farm is located on 196th Street; call (317) 776–0779 for exact directions.

If you appreciate cleanliness in the restaurant of your choice, try the Classic Kitchen in Noblesville. You could eat off the floor. Not only is the restaurant impeccably clean, it serves some of the best food in central Indiana. Its herb bread draws raves from customers, who sometimes opt for additional portions of bread instead of dessert. Not to put down the desserts—discerning diners, who come from miles around, heap accolades on the white chocolate mousse. Prices are moderate. Open 11:00 A.M. to 2:00 P.M. for lunch and 2:00 to 4:00 P.M. for tea, Tuesday through Saturday; candlelight dinner 6:00 to 9:00 P.M. Friday and Saturday. Located at 610 Hannibal Street; (317) 773–7385.

Hancock County

Hancock County is James Whitcomb Riley country. Here he was born, grew up, and found the inspiration for many of his poems, including such classics as "When the Frost is on the Punkin," "Little Orphant Annie," "The Raggedy Man," and "The Old Swimmin' Hole."

He was born on October 7, 1849, in what is now the kitchen of a white frame house built by Riley's father, who was an able carpenter in addition to being a lawyer noted for his oratory. Located at 250 West Main Street (Highway 40) in Greenfield, this house was immortalized in Riley's poems. It contains the rafter room where "the gobble-uns'll git you ef you don't watch out," the dining room "where they et on Sundays," and the side porch where Mary Alice Smith, who worked for the Riley family and is believed to have been the real-life "Little Orphant Annie," would "shoo the chickens off the porch." The house, complete with a collection of Riley memorabilia, is open to the public from 10:00 A.M. to 4:00 P.M. Monday through Saturday and 1:00 to 4:00 P.M. Sunday, May through October; nominal admission fee; (317) 462–8539.

Although Riley was a lifelong bachelor and never had children of his own, he dearly loved them, and they in turn loved him. The statue of the famous Hoosier poet seen today on the lawn of the Hancock County Courthouse (110 South State Street, Greenfield) was purchased entirely with funds contributed by the school children of Indiana.

Not far east of the Riley home, at the northwest corner of the intersection of Highway 40 and Apple Street, you'll find **Riley Memorial Park.** A boulder, into which are carved the words "Riley's Old Swimmin' Hole," stands on the banks of Brandywine Creek within the twenty-acre park and marks the exact spot where Riley and the friends of his youth once whiled away the hours on hot summer days. The youth of today frolic in a modern pool nearby. For additional information, contact the Greater Greenfield Chamber of Commerce, 110 South State Street, Greenfield, 46140; (317) 462–4188.

Although Riley eventually left Greenfield, he maintained his residence in Indiana until his death in 1916. You'll find his Indianapolis home and burial site described later in this section under Marion County.

Another place of interest in Riley Park is the two-story **Old Log Jail Museum.** Since log jails could hardly be called escape proof, their builders resorted to various ingenious methods to keep prisoners incarcerated. This jail features an upstairs cell room and logs filled with nails to keep prisoners from "sawing out." Nominal admission fee; (317) 462–4796.

If, some warm day, you are driving along County Road 300E just north of its intersection with County Road 400N, you may see a kangaroo bounding across the field next to you. Not to worry—you're not entering a time warp, another dimension, or the twilight zone. You're merely passing the **C. C. Irving Wild Game Farm,** where in addition to kangaroos, you're just as likely to see camels, peacocks, llamas, zebras, and other exotic wildlife roaming a fenced-in range during warm-weather months. The farm is not open to the public, but the wire fence permits excellent viewing from the road.

At the Irving Materials office, located approximately 5 miles northwest of the farm at the intersection of State Road 9 and State Road 234 near Eden, you can stop by the lobby any business day to see a collection of rare, stuffed animals. Contact Irving Materials, Inc., 8032 North State Road 9, Greenfield 46140; (317) 326–3101.

Johnson County

The **Johnson County Museum** is well worth the attention of area history buffs. Housed in a thirteen-room building, the mu-

Riley Memorial Park

seum displays more than 20,000 items, including antiques, Indian artifacts, guns, tools, and an interesting collection of nineteenth-century dresses. Four of its rooms have been furnished to depict the period between the Civil War and the turn of the century. But perhaps the most interesting (albeit a bit grisly) exhibit of all is a blood-spattered fan held by a woman who sat in Abraham Lincoln's box at the Ford Theater the night he was assassinated.

On the lawn outside the museum is an authentic log cabin built in 1835. It was discovered when an old house elsewhere in the county was being demolished—the house had been built around the cabin.

The museum, located at 150 West Madison in Franklin, is open from 1:00 to 4:00 P.M. and 7:00 to 8:00 P.M. on Thursday or at other times by appointment; (317) 736-4655.

You'll find numerous restaurants in Greenwood, but one of the finest is the Johnson County Line, situated at 1265 North Madison Avenue. Readers of *Indianapolis* Magazine recently rated this establishment the "Best Kept Secret" in central Indiana. They loved its prime rib, smoked salmon, steaks, large variety of appetizers, chocolate fondue, homemade cheesecakes, and atmosphere. If you'd like to find out for yourself what all the fuss is about, the Johnson County Line restaurant is open 5:00 to 9:00 P.M. Monday through Thursday, 5:00 to 11:00 P.M. Friday and Saturday, and 5:00 to 8:00 P.M. Sunday; (317) 887-0404.

Madison County

On the north side of the little country town of Chesterfield, two massive stone gateposts mark the entrance to the beautiful parklike grounds of **Camp Chesterfield.** They also mark the entrance to another world, for Camp Chesterfield is one of two major headquarters in this country for spiritualists (for you curious types, the other is at Lily Dale, New York).

Spiritualists, in case you don't have a dictionary handy, believe that mortals can communicate with the spirits of the dead through a medium. Using a variety of methods, the mediums at Camp Chesterfield attempt to do just that. They conduct seances, go into trances, evoke ectoplasms, cause spirits to materialize, and predict the future. The mediums are carefully screened before being selected to join the camp's staff, and each has his or her own specialty or specialties and sees clients by appointment

13

in one of the cottages scattered about the forty-eight-acre grounds.

Visitors are welcome from 9:00 A.M. to 5:00 P.M. daily and at other times for special events. Fees, quite reasonable, are charged for private consultations with the staff member of your choice, but there is no charge to enter the camp, attend services at the Cathedral in the Woods, view various public demonstrations of psychic phenomena, or tour the fascinating art gallery and museum. The last houses the memorabilia of the Fox Sisters, who are credited with initiating the movement of Modern Spiritualism.

If you'd like to read up on such subjects as reincarnation, astrology, and faith healing, you'll find books on these subjects and more in the camp's bookstore. A gourmet chef presides over a cafeteria that serves three meals a day, and several hotels offer overnight accommodations. There are even a few campsites for self-contained recreational vehicles. Occasionally, you can take courses in such subjects as ESP, the technique of spiritual healing, and numerology.

Lest you scoff, remember that such notables as Arthur Conan Doyle, creator of Sherlock Holmes, and Thomas Edison dabbled in spiritualism. Even Sigmund Freud expressed an interest in the movement and said shortly before his death that if he had his life to live over again he "would concern himself more with these matters." No matter what your beliefs, you will leave here with much food for thought. For a schedule of events and other information, write Camp Chesterfield, P.O. Box 132, Chesterfield 46017; (317) 378–0235. To make hotel reservations, write the Hotel Manager at the same address or call (317) 378–0237. The camp is located at the north end of Washington Street in the town of Chesterfield.

Not far southwest of Chesterfield, atop limestone bluffs overlooking the White River, you can study the curious architecture of some mound-building Indians. Of the eleven prehistoric earthworks preserved at **Mounds State Park,** the most exceptional is the circular Great Mound, nearly 1,200 feet in circumference and 9 feet high. Two other mounds are guitar-shaped, yet another conical, and one U-shaped. Some excavations may be seen, and a naturalist is available to explain the cultures of the Adena and Hopewell Indians, who are believed to have built these mounds. In addition to historical tours, the park offers a swimming pool, hiking and cross-country ski trails, modern campsites, and canoeing on the White River. Canoes and ski equipment may be rented in the park. You can reach the park by taking Mounds Road (State Road 232) southwest from Chesterfield for about 2 miles. There's a nominal vehicle admission fee from spring through fall. Write Mounds State Park, 4306 Mounds Road, Anderson 46013; (317) 642–6627.

The Church of God, with world headquarters at Anderson, has established **Anderson University** near the north edge of town. On campus is the ultramodern Warner Auditorium, noted for its architecture. Five days were required to lift its rounded roof, the largest thin-shelled concrete dome in the world, into place.

Elsewhere on campus, you can visit the Charles E. Wilson Library, which contains the archives and personal papers of the man who served as Secretary of Defense under President Eisenhower. The Wilson Art Gallery houses a $250,000 porcelain bird collection donated by Wilson's daughter and a collection of 1,500 napkin rings that range in variety from a solid gold, jewel-encrusted ring once used by Louis XIV of France to rings made from toilet paper spools in a Japanese prison camp during World War II. More than 10,000 artifacts from the Holy Land are displayed in the Bible Museum, and Reardon Auditorium contains an unusual chandelier that holds some 10,000 light bulbs. During summer months, the National Football League's Indianapolis Colts can be seen practicing on a campus field. The college is located at the corner of East Fifth Street and College Drive; (317) 649–9071.

Marion County

If anyone ever compiles a list of national treasures, the Indianapolis Children's Museum should be on it. It is the largest children's museum in the world, and in this case, bigger *is* better. You can ride a turn-of-the-century carousel, explore the twisting passages of a limestone cave, visit a log cabin, an Indian tepee, an igloo, and an Egyptian tomb inhabited by the 3,000-year-old mummy of a princess, stand beside a fifty-five-ton wood-burning locomotive, watch a spectacular collection of toy trains in motion, examine replicas of prehistoric creatures, and conduct scientific experiments. If you can coax the adults away from it, your child can sit behind the wheel of 1940 Maserati that once competed in the Indy 500. Other exhibits, such as the computer center, provide a bridge to the future. Even the museum's restaurant carries out the see, touch, and do theme—you can stand at a window and watch the bakers make such goodies as croissants and cookies. A planetarium, included in a new addition currently under construction, is scheduled to open late in 1988.

The five-level museum nourishes all those qualities we cherish in our children—a sense of wonder, curiosity, imagination, the desire to know and to create, and the ability to dream. And if you don't have a child, come anyway; this is an enchanting place for anyone.

General admission is free, but there's a small charge for riding the carousel. Museum and restaurant hours are 10:00 A.M. to 5:00 P.M. Monday through Saturday and noon to 5:00 P.M. Sunday; closed major winter holidays and on Mondays from the day after Labor Day to the week before Memorial Day. The carousel operates from 2:00 to 5:00 P.M. on school days and during regular museum hours other days. You'll find the museum at the corner of 30th and Meridian streets; (317) 924–5431.

The **Indianapolis Museum of Art,** situated on a bluff overlooking the White River, is far more than a museum. It's a 154-acre art park that includes a sculpture garden, botanical gardens, patches of woodland, greenhouses, a wildlife refuge, and a fine restaurant. Among its exhibits are the largest collection of J. M. W. Turner watercolors in the United States, important collections of textiles and Oriental art, and a self-portrait of Rembrandt as a young man. The museum site was once the private estate of Mr. and Mrs. J. K. Lilly, Jr. (of Lilly pharmaceutical fame), and there is also much of architectural interest here. The main exhibition buildings are open, free of charge, 11:00 A.M. to 5:00 P.M. Tuesday through Sunday; fee for special exhibitions. A donation is requested at the Lilly Pavilion (the original Lilly mansion), which is open 1:00 to 4:00 P.M. Tuesday through Sunday. Many special events and programs are held here. Visitors may purchase a wide variety of flowering bulbs and plants at the greenhouses (open 11:00 A.M. to 5:00 P.M. Tuesday through Sunday) and used art objects, clothing, and furniture at the Better-Than-New Shop (open noon to 4:00 P.M. Tuesday through Saturday). The museum is located at 1200 West 38th Street; (317) 923–1331.

Indianapolis is going wild over its new state-of-the-art zoo, a model for zoos of the future, which opened to the public in June 1988. Stretching along the west bank of the White River, the innovative sixty-four-acre facility is the first zoo ever to be completely designed around the biome concept. Biomes are simulated natural environments in which animals are grouped by habitats rather than by the continents of their origins. Forest animals from around the world, for instance, share the forest biome, while other animals find appropriate homes in the desert, plains, and water biomes. Unlike most of its counterparts, the **Indianapolis Zoo** combines the best elements of a zoo and an aquarium, with particular emphasis on a marine exhibit that has been called the best of its kind outside of Sea World. The totally enclosed Whale and Dolphin Pavilion, largest in the world, presents animal shows every day of the year, while a vast aquarium offers above- and below-water views of some 200 aquatic species. Only five zoos in the world possess the capabilities to exhibit walruses—this zoo is one of them. Among the things you *won't* find here are cages and bars. Animals and people watch one another across such natural barriers as moats and boulders and, where necessary, through meshwork that disappears as you look at it. One resident giraffe graphically requested a special privilege for his brethren by licking a hole through the wall of the giraffe barn—the barn is now equipped with windows 14 feet above the ground so that the lanky creatures can have a home with a view. Open daily 9:00 A.M. to 8:30 P.M. (gate closes at 7:00 P.M.) April through Labor Day, 9:00 A.M. to 5:30 P.M. (gate closes at 4:00 P.M.) rest of year; admission fee (reduced rate from 9:00 to 11:00 A.M. on the first Tuesday of each month). The zoo is located just west of the downtown area at 1200 West Washington Street; (317) 630–2030 or 638–8072.

The new zoo lies within 267-acre White River State Park, which borders both sides of the waterway for which it is named. To view drawings and a model of what White River State Park is envisioned to become during the next few years and to obtain up-to-date information about planned facilities, stop at the park's Visitors Center at 801 West Washington Street. Open 8:00 A.M. to 5:00 P.M. Monday through Friday; (317) 634–4567.

Eagle Creek Park is the home of the Museum of Indian Heritage, filled with rare arts and crafts created through the centuries by American Indians. When Sitting Bull's great nephew, Tatanka Iyotake Hoksila, visited here, he described it as "the most authentic collection I've seen in my lifetime." A gift shop on the premises sells items crafted by modern-day Indians. Museum hours are 10:00 A.M. to 5:00 P.M. Tuesday through Sunday; closed Monday and major holidays; nominal admission fee. The museum is at 6040 Delong Road; (317) 293–4488.

17

One of the largest city parks in the country, Eagle Creek includes 3,800 acres of rolling terrain and a 1,300-acre reservoir. Its nature center houses an injured animal nursery. Nearby is an arboretum that boasts a 400-year-old Douglas fir log and a beech tree into which Daniel Boone once carved his still-visible initials. (If you wonder why the carving is so high up, naturalists surmise it's because Boone was on horseback when he left his mark there.) Much of the park's summertime appeal centers on Eagle Creek Reservoir, which features a three-acre swimming beach, pontoon boat cruises, the only internationally sanctioned canoe/kayak regatta course in the country (site of the 1988 U.S. Olympic trials), and a marina that rents boats, canoes, and sailboards. Also in the park are hiking, bicycling, and cross-country ski trails, an eighteen-hole golf course, a jogger's outdoor exercise course, a world-class archery field, ice-skating ponds, and sled runs. The park is open dawn to dusk every day of the year; a nominal entrance fee is slightly higher on Saturday and Sunday. Enter the park at 7840 West 56th Street; (317) 293–4827.

A marvelous getaway spot, especially in the winter, is the serene world within the walls of the **Garfield Park Conservatory.** Outside, the world may be white with snow, but inside, it is summer eternally. Vividly colored birds live among trees that shade giant ferns and lush vegetation. Tropical fish swim in a series of pools fed by a 15-foot waterfall. Walk beneath the falls and enter the environs of the desert, not barren at all, but alive with cacti, succulents, and carnivorous plants. Outside, from May through October, the sunken gardens are brilliant with hundreds of blooms. Garfield Park is located at 2450 South Shelby Street; open daily dawn to dusk; free. The conservatory is open 10:00 A.M. to 5:00 P.M. Tuesday through Saturday and noon to 5:00 P.M. Sunday, with special hours for seasonal shows; free admission on Tuesday, nominal fee other days; (317) 784–3044.

Holliday Park would certainly be a top contender for honors as Indianapolis's most unusual park. Located on the west bank of the White River at 6349 Spring Mill Road, the eighty-acre park was initially developed in 1936 as a botanical garden, and the grounds still contain more than 800 species of plants. The park is most noted, however, for its "ruins."

Three stone statues that formerly resided on the now-vanished St. Paul Building in New York City rest on a pedestal atop Doric columns, dominating a setting that is the focal point of Holliday Park. Three times life size, the kneeling figures represent a white, black, and Asian who have labored in unity. Just behind the statues, contributing to the ruins effect, are twenty-seven columns, each 10 feet tall, that were obtained from a local convent when it was razed a few years back. Open daily dawn to dusk; free; (317) 253–5383.

Until 1982, Indianapolis's grand old Union Station stood virtually empty, a decaying monument to the glory days of the railroad. Today, after $50 million worth of painstaking renovation, it is a festival marketplace where people can view architecture restored to its original splendor, shop, eat, enjoy free entertainment, and even stay overnight. Among the more than one hundred shops, restaurants, and nightclubs located here is the NBC Store, currently one of only three in the country, where fans can pick up T-shirts and souvenirs imprinted with logos from the television network's shows (items bearing the name of Indianapolis-born David Letterman are best-sellers). The Magic Shop sells packaged illusions of all sorts and sizes, including cabinets in which hapless victims can be sawed in half, for both amateur and professional magicians. No child will protest spending time at the Midway, which offers classic state fair rides and games indoors—the bumper cars are well nigh irresistible. At ultramodern IND*EX (The Indiana Experience Museum), visitors can sample the best the Hoosier State has to offer—shoot free throws in an area honoring Indiana basketball; listen to the words of such famous native sons as James Whitcomb Riley and James Dean, here represented as talking statues; examine a 1911 Auburn touring car; and wander Indiana via videotapes. A 276-room Holiday Inn with a railroad theme occupies a former train shed and features twenty-six suites in vintage Pullman railroad cars. The Union Station complex, located south of Georgia Street, spans two city blocks from Capitol Avenue on the west to Meridian Street on the east. Union Station is open 10:00 A.M. to 10:00 P.M. Monday through Thursday and some holidays, 10:00 A.M. to 11:00 P.M. Friday and Saturday, noon to 8:00 P.M. Sunday, April through September and mid-November through December; 10:00 A.M. to 9:00 P.M. Monday through Thursday and some holidays, 10:00 A.M. to 10:00 P.M. Friday and Saturday, 11:00 A.M. to 7:00 P.M. Sunday, rest of year; closed major winter holidays; facility hours vary. Contact Union Station Associates, Department of Transportation and Tourism, 39 West Jackson Place, Indianapolis 46225; (317) 637–1888 or 635–7955. Oh, yes, you can also catch a train at Union Station. Amtrak provides daily round trips to Chicago; call (317) 632–1905 or 1–800–872–7245 for schedule and rates.

In the midst of Lockerbie Square, a six-block area of late-nineteenth-century homes near downtown Indianapolis, stands an old brick house once occupied by poet James Whitcomb Riley (for information about Riley's birthplace, see Hancock County in this section). Riley spent the last twenty-three years of his life here, and his memorabilia are everywhere. The structure, built in 1872, is recognized as one of the two best Victorian preservations in the country. Nothing here has been restored to the way someone thought it should look—this is history untouched. Riley's pen is on his desk, his suits are in the closet, and a hat is on the bed. The carpets are slightly faded, and the upholstery shows signs of wear, just as when Riley lived here and when he left here. A humble, unpretentious man, Riley would have been astounded to learn that his home is now a major tourist attraction, luring visitors from sixteen countries in a recent two-month period. Located at 528 Lockerbie Street, the home is open 10:00 A.M.to 4:00 P.M. Tuesday through Saturday and noon to 4:00 P.M. Sunday; closed major holidays; nominal admission fee. For additional information, write the James Whitcomb Riley Memorial Association, 11 South Meridian Street, Suite 606, Indianapolis 46204; (317) 631–5885.

When Riley died in 1916, he was interred in Crown Hill Cemetery. His grave, sheltered by an elegant but simple Greek temple, is at the crest of Strawberry Hill, the highest point in Indianapolis.

Among the other notables buried here are Benjamin Harrison, twenty-third president of the United States; three vice-presidents; and the infamous John Dillinger. Ironically, it is Dillinger's grave that commands the most attention. His funeral in 1934 was the only occasion in Crown Hill's history when the cemetery had to close its gates and restrict attendance. In the years since, it has been necessary to replace his grave marker several times. Souvenir hunters chip away at them relentlessly, and one collector actually carried away an entire tombstone.

Also located here is the Crown Hill National Cemetery—a cemetery within a cemetery and the final resting place for nearly 2,000 soldiers, mostly Civil War veterans. The cemetery's main gate at 3402 Boulevard Place is open daily during daylight hours. Before entering, however, you should stop by the office at 700 West 38th Street and ask for a map and/or directions to the various gravesites; the cemetery covers more than 500 acres and is crisscrossed by 50 miles of roads. Open daily 8:30 A.M. to 4:00 P.M.; (317) 925–8231.

Well-traveled deli connoisseurs will tell you that Shapiro's Delicatessen in southside Indianapolis is the equal of any in New York or Chicago. Believe them! Shapiro's has been a much-loved local fixture since 1905, growing through the years and several generations of Shapiros from a small grocery store with a few tables into a deli/restaurant that serves approximately 2,500 devotees each day. You'll find all the usual deli fare here and then some, generously served, moderately priced, and deliciously prepared. The corned beef, made from a family recipe that won a blue ribbon at the 1939 World's Fair in New York City, sells by the ton—about three tons a week, to be exact. Other highly rated treats include matzo ball and vegetable soups, pastrami sandwiches, potato pancakes, liver pâté, pickled herring, and, on Sundays only, *real* mashed potatoes. Don't forget the desserts—food critics and just plain eaters rank them with the best Indianapolis has to offer. The strawberry-topped and chocolate cheesecakes are without peer. Breakfast, lunch, and dinner are served every day of the week (eat in or carry out); open 6:30 A.M. to 8:30 P.M. Located at 808 South Meridian Street; (317) 631–4041. A smaller northside Shapiro's, established during recent years at 2370 West 86th Street, is open during the same hours; (317) 872–7255.

On the east side of Indianapolis, it's not uncommon to see whole families lined up outside waiting to get into the Paramount Music Palace, a combination restaurant and showplace. The pizza, lasagna, salad bar, and old-fashioned soda fountain treats, all low to moderately priced, are reason enough to come here, but the big drawing card is Paramount's spectacular theatre pipe organ. This is no ordinary organ, mind you. This gleaming ebony organ has more than 3,400 pipes and can evoke the sounds of more than forty different instruments—an entire orchestra unto itself. Two highly qualified organists alternate musical interludes of twenty minutes with ten-minute breaks. The Paramount Music Palace is open 11:00 A.M. to 2:00 P.M. and 5:00 to 10:00 P.M. Tuesday through Thursday; 11:00 A.M. to 2:00 P.M. and 5:00 to 11:00 P.M. Friday, 11:30 A.M. to 11:00 P.M. Saturday, and 11:30 to 9:00 P.M. Sunday. It is also open 5:00 to 11:00 P.M. some Monday evenings in summer months. Located at 7560 Old Trails Road, southwest of the intersection of Interstate 465 and Highway 40 (East Washington Street); (317) 352–0144.

Just west of Indianapolis is the **Indianapolis Motor Speedway,** where each May the world-famous Indy 500 auto race is held. When the course is not being used for competition or test purposes, you can see the track as professional racers see it by taking a bus tour around the 2¹/₂-mile asphalt oval. Your pace, of course, will be much more leisurely, and you'll learn many interesting facts along the way.

A **Hall of Fame Museum** inside the track houses a vast collection of racing, classic, and antique passenger cars, including more than thirty past winners of the Indy 500, and some valuable, jewel-encrusted trophies. Perhaps the best-known artifact is the unusual Borg-Warner Trophy, which displays the sculptured, three-dimensional faces of every 500 winner since 1936.

The museum and track, located at 4790 West 16th Street in the suburb of Speedway, are open 9:00 A.M. to 5:00 P.M. daily, year-round, except Christmas. A nominal fee is charged for both the museum and the track tour; tour information and tickets are available at the museum; (317) 241–2500.

Indianapolis, which has a well-deserved reputation for being the amateur sports capital of the country, recently became the new home of the National Track and Field Hall of Fame. Among the exhibits are a track shoe worn by the legendary Jesse Owens, a hurdle used in 1884, a photographic tribute to Jim Thorpe, and an unfinished poster publicizing the 1940 Olympics in Tokyo (canceled because of an impending World War II). Located at 200 South Capitol Avenue in the Hoosier Dome, home of the National Football League's Indianapolis Colts, the Hall of Fame is open 11:00 A.M. to 5:00 P.M. daily except during some Dome events and on major holidays; nominal admission fee; (317) 261–0483.

Fort Benjamin Harrison is the home of the U.S. Army's huge Financial and Accounting Center, which each month issues nearly $2 billion worth of payroll checks to army personnel around the world. Off the front (north) lobby of the sprawling structure that contains the Center is the U.S. Army Finance Corps Museum, where visitors can see such monetary mementos as World War II prisoner-of-war canteen chits, counterfeit paper money from Korea and the Philippines, financial notes from the Revolutionary War era, and a wide variety of foreign currency. Open 8:00 A.M. to 4:30 P.M. Monday through Friday, except federal holidays; free; (317) 542–2169. It is on the northeast side of Indianapolis. To reach the museum, enter through the fort's west gate, which lies on East 56th Street approximately 2 miles east of exit 39 on Interstate 465; look for signs.

The state's first medical center, housed in the Old Pathology Building on the grounds of Central State Hospital, remains virtually untouched by time. Now Known as the Indiana Medical History Museum, it features a fascinating collection of some 10,000 medical artifacts used in the nineteenth and early twentieth centuries. Free; open 1:00 to 4:00 P.M. Wednesday and other times by appointment. Located at 3000 West Washington Street in Indianapolis; (317) 635–7329.

Twinkie lovers can watch the spongy treats being made, along with Ding Dongs, doughnuts, and other goodies, at the Wonder and Hostess Bakery in Indianapolis. Best of all, the free tours conclude with free samples, coffee or milk, and even some take-home snacks. Located at 2929 North Shadeland Avenue; call (317) 547–9421 for tour hours.

Morgan County

At any given time, the goldfish population of Martinsville outnumbers the human population about one hundred to one. The goldfish make their home in the spring-fed ponds and tanks of **Grassyfork Fisheries, Inc.,** which covers 1,500 acres and is believed to be the largest goldfish hatchery in the world. More than 40 million fish, from fantails to the showy shubunkins, are produced here each year and shipped all over the world. Grassyfork is also a major producer of water lilies, and when they bloom on display ponds during warm-weather months, the landscape looks like a Monet painting come to life.

Although Grassyfork is a wholesale operation, the management will sometimes sell you a fish or two if you bring along your own container. There are no guided tours, but visitors are welcome to view the ponds and observe the sorting and packing operations any business day of the year. Hours are 8:30 to 11:00 A.M. and noon to 4:00 P.M. Monday through Friday and 8:00 to 11:00 A.M. Saturday. The hatchery is located at 2906 East Morgan Street; (317) 342–4127.

As a little boy, Elliott Drake was fascinated with phonographs. As a grown man, he gathered together one of the world's finest collections of antique phonographs, and you can see them all at the **Midwest Phonograph Museum** in Martinsville. Every type of talking machine imaginable is here—an 1898 Columbia Phonograph with eleven sets of listening tubes so the whole family could listen together (this machine could only be heard through a tube), an electric lamp phonograph that was popular in the Roaring Twenties (the top of the lamp shade lifts up to reveal a turn-table), an 1858 phonautograph (the oldest machine in the museum), and a Bell and Tainter Graphophone, vintage 1886, which uses cardboard recordings. More than 300 machines are kept on permanent display, with 300 more brought out from time to time as part of a changing exhibit.

The museum is open 2:00 to 7:00 P.M. on Saturday, Sunday, and some holidays; other times upon request. It stands at 2255 State Road 252, just off State Road 37, in Martinsville; a large sign is in the front yard. Nominal admission charge; (317) 342–7666.

If you're the type whose curiosity is piqued by life's mysteries, head for Mooresville and nearby **Gravity Hill.** Legend has it that an Indian witch doctor was buried long ago at the foot of this low hill, and the great energy and power he possessed in life still emanates from the good doctor's grave. Anyone who stops his car at the bottom of the hill and puts it in neutral will find himself coasting backwards up the slope for nearly a quarter of a mile. Don't scoff until you've tried it—witch doctor or no, it really works! Gravity Hill is located on Keller Hill Road, which runs west off State Road 42 on the south side of Mooresville; for exact directions, ask local residents or contact the Mooresville Chamber of Commerce, 26 South Indiana Street (P.O. Box 62), Mooresville 46158; (317) 831–6509.

Astronomers from Indiana University in Bloomington travel to Mooresville to keep an eye on happenings in the universe. That's where the **Goethe Link Observatory** is situated. On certain nights in spring and fall, the general public may share the astronomers' view through the observatory's 36-inch reflector and 10-inch refractor telescopes and hear a lecture that describes current astronomical highlights in laymen's terms. For a schedule, reservations, and free tickets (necessary for admission), write Public Night, Astronomy Department, Swain Hall West, Room 319, Indiana University, Bloomington 47405, or call (812) 337–6911.

Sharing the one hundred-acre grounds of the Link estate with the observatory are the fifteen-acre **Link Daffodil Gardens,** resplendent with blooms for about two weeks in late April. They're open daily, free of charge, during daylight hours. Ms. Link, a nationally recognized authority on the daffodil, raises an array of different types here and is happy to share her garden with visitors. You may call (317) 831–3283 to check blooming times or watch for an announcement in the Indianapolis newspapers. The Link estate lies just off State Road 67 about 5 miles south of

Mooresville near the tiny community of Brooklyn; follow observatory signs.

An eye-catching house in Morgantown has for many years been luring architects, geologists, and just plain folks from across the nation. Built between 1894 and 1896 as a private residence, the house is adorned with the turrets, gables, and cones that were popular in the Victorian era, but there any similarity to other houses of its times ends. The walls are constructed of concrete blocks, imbedded on the exterior with rocks and geodes of all shapes and sizes, bits of colored glass, seashells, Indian relics, jewelry, marbles, doll heads, keys, and even a picture of two puppies under glass. Since the original owner kept enlarging the house to accommodate a family that eventually included twenty-two children, many of the items on the walls depict segments of family history. Today, the fanciful house is a bed-and-breakfast inn that welcomes guests for $35–$55 a night. Contact the **Rock House Inn,** 380 West Washington Street, Morgantown 46160; (812) 597-5100.

Shelby County

An extraordinary dining experience awaits you in Morristown. Nestled amid some lovely gardens, the Kopper Kettle is as much a museum as a restaurant. It occupies a picturesque, nineteenth-century manor house accented with stained-glass windows and filled with antiques and art objects from around the world. All this beauty should be regarded as a free bonus, because the meal awaiting you inside would be unforgettable served in any surroundings.

The wide range of entrees changes somewhat from day to day, but you can't go wrong with fried chicken, steak, or seafood. All side dishes are served family style, and you're encouraged to ask for refills. You won't find anything really fancy here—just plain food distinguished by perfect preparation, moderate prices, and elegant atmosphere.

Located at 135 West Main Street (Highway 52), the Kopper Kettle is open for lunch from 11:00 A.M. to 3:00 P.M. Tuesday through Saturday. The dinner menu is available from 11:00 A.M. to 8:30 P.M. Tuesday through Saturday and from 11:00 A.M. to 6:30 P.M. on Sunday; closed Monday. Reservations are recommended; (317) 763-6767.

Tiny Boggstown was, until recently, just another rural Indiana community—a pleasant place to be, but in no way distinctive. In July 1984, however, that all changed. That's when the Boggstown Inn & Cabaret opened for business, and the "joint has been jumping" ever since. At last count, folks from every state in the Union and from more than twenty-five countries (including Russia, Thailand, and Australia) have trekked to the Boggstown Inn for a nostalgic dose of ragtime music. Performers may include piano, banjo, or washboard players, a small band, or singers (a different combination is offered each evening), but the show always features a sing-along. The inn opens for dinner at 6:00 P.M.; the music begins at 7:00 P.M. and continues nonstop until the inn closes at about 11:00 P.M. Entertainment charges vary, depending on whether or not you dine there, what time you arrive, and what night you come. Open Wednesday through Saturday; dinner prices range from $10–$16 on Friday and Saturday and from $7–$14 on Wednesday and Thursday. Reservations are a must and should be made well ahead of your visit (from four to six weeks for the slightly more popular nights of Friday and Saturday). Since few of the roads leading to Boggstown are marked on any map, you'll be sent directions for getting there when you make your reservation. Write the inn at R.R. 1, Box 38, Boggstown 46110, or call (317) 835–2020. The inn also offers a Sunday brunch to the accompaniment of live piano music; no reservations required (call for hours). During the first week in August, the inn stages a six-night-long Hoosier Ragtime Festival.

Off the Beaten Path in Northeast Indiana

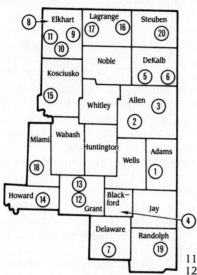

1. Amishville, U.S.A./First Mennonite Church
2. Children's Zoo/Louis A. Warren Lincoln Library and Museum/Lakeside Rose Garden
3. Grabill Country Fair
4. Glory of the Sea Museum
5. Auburn-Cord-Duesenberg Museum
6. Ralph Sechler & Son pickle factory
7. Ball State University/Christy Woods/Wishon-Harrell Pottery Place
8. Midwest Museum of American Art
9. Deutsch Kase Haus
10. Amish Acres
11. Bird's-Eye View Museum
12. Park Cemetery/James Dean Fairmount Historical Museum
13. Easter pageant
14. Elwood Haynes Museum/Big Ben/Kokomo Opalescent Glass Co.
15. concrete egg/Lawrence D. Bell Aircraft Museum
16. Tamarack Bog State Nature Preserve
17. Shipshewana Auction and Flea Market/Menno-Hof Visitors Center
18. Circus City Museum/Mount Hope Cemetery/Grissom Air Force Base
19. Silver Towne Coin Shop/ International Hawaiian Steel Guitar Convention
20. Pokagon State Park/ Potawatomi State Nature Preserve

Northeast Indiana

Adams County

Just south of Berne, you can drive through a picturesque covered bridge across the Wabash River and leave the twentieth century behind. You are now in the land of the Amish, where windmills replace skyscrapers and horse-drawn buggies move sedately along dusty country roads. This is the home of **Amishville, U.S.A.,** a 120-acre Amish farm open to the public.

While the resident family goes about its daily business of managing the farm, using the century-old methods of their ancestors, visitors stroll through the barn, milk house, smoke house, wash house, and old-fashioned garden. Modern conveniences have no place here: the Amish live their lives without motors, plumbing, refrigeration, radios, televisions, and automobiles. At Amishville, you can learn all about the simple life-style these gentle people have embraced by choice.

Entrance is free, but nominal fees are charged for a guided tour of the authentic Amish house and outbuildings and for buggy rides and hayrides in the summer and sleigh rides in the winter. In deference to both Amish tradition and the Swiss heritage of surrounding communities, Der Essen Platz (The Eating Place) at Amishville serves home-cooked foods that are favorites of both cultures. Two small lakes are available for fishing, swimming, and, in the winter, ice-skating. For those who want to stay a spell and let the peace sink in, there's a large wooded campground.

You can reach Amishville by going south from Berne on Highway 27 for 3 miles; at County Road 950S, turn east and follow the signs. Open daily from 9:00 A.M. to 5:00 P.M. Monday through Saturday; 1:00 to 5:00 P.M. Sunday; guided tours available daily April through November. Write Amishville, U.S.A., RR 2, Box 255, Geneva 46740; (219) 589–3536.

In the Swiss village of Berne, you can visit the **First Mennonite Church.** Located at the intersection of Highway 27 and State Road 218, the classic Gothic structure is one of the two largest Mennonite churches in North America. Some 2,000 people can be seated in the main sanctuary. The church is open to visitors daily from 9:00 A.M. to 4:30 P.M.; Sunday services are held at 10:00 A.M.; (219) 589–3108.

Amishville, U.S.A.

For information about Berne's unusual shops and stores, many of which cater to the area's 4,000 Amish residents, contact the Berne Chamber of Commerce, P.O. Box 85, Berne 46711; (219) 589–2784. Information is also available at the Tourist Center in Yodeling Village, 105 West Water Street; (219) 589–8982.

A turn-of-the-century aura of a different sort is found in Decatur. The Back 40 Junction, famous for both food and decor, is housed in a country railroad station. Outside, on remnant stretches of train track, you can view such railroad memorabilia as a 1920s-era club car, complete with original lighting fixtures, seats, and berths. The "little red caboose" is a gift shop. Inside the station is a fine restaurant decorated with hundreds of antiques and bits of Americana. Antique oil lamps that once belonged to actress Carole Lombard are here, as well as a Tiffany chandelier, an old ox yoke, and a collection of the Burma Shave signs that once lined our nation's highways and provided many a laugh. Although the Back 40 Junction offers a regular lunch and dinner menu, it is the moderately priced smorgasbord that has brought it fame. It's served from 11:00 A.M. to 2:00 P.M. Monday through Saturday; 3:30 to 9:00 P.M. Monday through Friday; 3:00 to 10:00 P.M. Saturday; and 11:00 A.M. to 7:00 P.M. Sundays and holidays; closed Christmas. Sing-alongs are a Friday night special. It is located at 1011 North 13th Street (Highway 27/33) on the north side of Decatur. Reservations accepted; (219) 724–3355.

Allen County

John Chapman, better known as Johnny Appleseed, traveled on foot through much of the Midwest, planting seeds that would one day grow into vast apple orchards. In his own time, he was much beloved, and he remains a folk hero to this day. What most folks don't realize is that Johnny didn't wander about in all those raggedy clothes because he had to. Johnny was a miser—kindly, but a miser nevertheless—who found free room and board with families along the routes he followed, planted some apple seeds in their fields, and eventually moved on. It was no surprise to those who knew him, then, that his death on March 18, 1845, was due to exposure. He died in Fort Wayne and was buried there with honors. His grave site, open at all times, is located in Archer Park on the east side of Parnell Avenue and just north of the St. Joseph River.

The thirty-eight-acre **Children's Zoo** with more than 500 domestic and exotic animals, delights visitors of all ages. Although small, it has been internationally recognized for its landscaping and cleverly designed exhibits. Children love to feed the animals, pet tame deer, and ride the miniature train; the whole family will love the safari through a re-created African Veldt where all animals roam free. A recently opened exhibit devoted to Australian wildlife, the largest of its kind in North America, includes a 20,000-gallon Great Barrier Reef aquarium. Open 9:00 A.M. to 8:00 P.M. daily in July; 9:00 A.M. to 5:00 P.M. Monday through Saturday; 9:00 A.M. to 6:00 P.M. Sundays and holidays, late April through June and August to mid-October. Admission fee. Located at 3411 Sherman Street in Fort Wayne's Franke Park; (219) 482–4610.

Believed to contain the world's largest private collection of literature devoted to one man, the **Louis A. Warren Lincoln Library and Museum** includes some 10,000 books in twenty-six languages dealing exclusively with Lincoln; paintings, letters, and personal possessions of the family; and such curios as the flag that draped Lincoln's box at the Ford Theatre. A remarkable collection of some 400 pictures of the sixteenth president and his descendants, the existence of which was known only to family members for many decades, was acquired by the museum after the death in 1985 of the last of the Lincolns (the president's great-grandson Robert Beckwith). Maps are available for a self-guided tour. The exhibits may be viewed free of charge from 8:30 A.M. to 4:30 P.M. Monday through Friday and 10:00 A.M. to 4:30 P.M. Saturday, mid-May through Labor Day; from 8:00 A.M. to 4:30 P.M. Monday through Thursday and 8:00 A.M. to 12:30 P.M. Friday, the rest of the year; closed holidays; Located on the main floor of the Lincoln National Life Insurance building at 1300 South Clinton Street in Fort Wayne; (219) 427–3864.

One of the most breathtaking sights in downtown Fort Wayne is the Foellinger-Freimann Botanical Conservatory, a series of three buildings connected by tunnels and one of the largest passive solar structures in the United States. Some 1,300 panels of insulating glass permit the sunshine to enter, and to ensure that all available sunlight could reach the buildings unimpeded, the city passed special zoning laws. Visitors will see special displays of North American desert plants, rare tropical plants from around the world, and changing seasonal exhibits. Nominal admission fee. Open 10:00 A.M. to 5:00 P.M. Monday through Saturday; noon to 4:00 P.M. Sundays and holidays; closed Christmas. Located at 1100 South Calhoun Street; (219) 422–3696.

Lakeside Rose Garden, which covers more than three acres, is Indiana's only All-America Rose Selection Display Garden. Currently, some 220 varieties flourish on nearly 2,500 labeled rose bushes against a backdrop of a lagoon, reflecting pools, and a Grecian-style pergolis. The blooms are glorious from June to mid-October, but the scenic grounds are open daily throughout the year during daylight hours. Free; located in Lakeside City Park at the corner of East Lake Avenue and Forest Park Boulevard; (219) 427–1270, 422–3696.

Anyone interested in architecture will want to see the Cathedral of the Immaculate Conception, a Gothic-style church in the center of Fort Wayne. Its Bavarian stained-glass windows are recognized as the finest in the Western Hemisphere, and its hand-carved wood altar is considered one of the finest wood carvings in the country. Maps are available for self-guided tours. Open 10:00 A.M.-2:00 P.M. Wednesday and Thursday and the second and fourth Sundays of each month; other times by appointment. Located at 1121 South Calhoun Boulevard; (219) 424–1485.

Other notable architectural sights are the campus buildings at Concordia Theological Seminary, designed by Eero Saarinen to resemble an early German moor village. They have won numerous national and worldwide awards for both design and landscaping. Contact the Seminary Relations Department on the campus at 6600 North Clinton Street in Fort Wayne for a free tour; (219) 482–9611.

The campus of St. Francis College boasts a college library housed in a mansion that was a residential showplace in the early 1900s. A stairway that spirals to the third floor of the thirty-three-room Romanesque structure is truly magnificent. A map and self-guided cassette tour describe the lavish wall hangings, hand-painted murals, and period rooms. Located at 2701 Spring Street in Fort Wayne; admission fee. Open daily except on school holidays during academic year, but hours vary; (219) 432–3551, extension 263.

Indiana's most honored gourmet restaurant—the Cafe Johnell in Fort Wayne—has won front-page notices in the *Wall Street Journal* and the *Chicago Tribune*, the Travel/Holiday Magazine Award for Dining Distinction (more than twenty consecutive years), the Mobil Guide Four Star Award, and the Ordre Du Merite Agricole from the Republic of France. In 1984, it was the only

Indiana restaurant chosen by *Playboy* Magazine as one of the country's one hundred finest. With recommendations like that, most anything you select should provide a real taste treat. The cuisine, of course, is decidedly French, and the owners say that among their current selections *sole amandine de Dover, caneton à l'orange flambé,* and *tournedos de boeuf Rossini* are customer favorites. (Now you have a chance to translate before visiting there.) The chef guarantees that you can cut all steaks with a fork, and the food is complemented by a notable art collection. Lunches range from $4.95–$14, dinners from $10–$30—prices that are a bit trendy for Indiana, but a bargain most places. Open for lunch 11:00 A.M. to 2:30 P.M. Monday through Friday; for dinner, 6:00 to 10:00 P.M. Monday through Friday and 5:00 to 11:00 P.M. Saturday; closed Sundays and major holidays. Located at 2529 South Calhoun Street; (219) 456–1939.

For a get-away-from-it-all experience, travel southwest from downtown Fort Wayne to Fox Island County Park. There, in a 270-acre state nature preserve, you'll see a 40-foot sand dune and a quaking bog whose surface ripples when you stamp your feet. Located at 7324 Yohne Road; (219) 747–7846.

The peaceful little town of Grabill, northeast of Fort Wayne, is a lovely place to explore crafts and antique shops. Each year, on the weekend following Labor Day, the **Grabill Country Fair** that lures people from throughout the Midwest. The fun includes contests for seed spitting, frog jumping, chicken flying, and wife calling. Go north from Fort Wayne on State Road 1 to Hosler Road in the town of Leo, then turn east on Hosler Road. For additional information, contact the Grabill Chamber of Commerce, P.O. Box 129, Grabill 46741; (219) 627–2012.

Blackford County

The nearest body of water of any sizable dimension is the Missinewa River, and that's not even in the same county. Yet here in landlocked Hartford City is an amazing collection of what's claimed to be the most sea and river shells in any museum anywhere. There are eighteen rooms in the **Glory of the Sea Museum,** filled with shells, sea life, and other sea-related items. Some shells are one-of-a-kind, freaks of nature. Others, such as the golden cowries, the chambered nautilus, and the glory of the seas (from which the museum takes its name) are extremely rare.

A giant clam shell weighs in at 250 pounds, while 1 million smaller seashells occupy two "wonder boxes." To help pay expenses, owner Fred Glancy sells some of his more common shells.

In addition to shells, you'll see semiprecious stones, fluorescent rocks, Indian crafts and artifacts, and a piece of Skylab that landed in Australia. The museum is free to youngsters in the eighth grade or younger, but older visitors are asked to purchase at least $2 worth of shells. Open 10:00 A.M. to 6:00 P.M. daily, June through November; by appointment in May and December. To reach the museum, go north from Hartford City on State Road 3; when you reach County Road 200N, turn west and proceed 1 1/4 miles to 1223 West 200N; look for museum sign. Contact Glory of the Sea Museum, RR 2, Hartford City 47348; (317) 348-3439.

DeKalb County

A rare treats awaits old car buffs in the town of Auburn. Housed in the administration building of the old Auburn Automobile Company is one of the country's finest collections of cars.

The **Auburn-Cord-Duesenberg Museum** and its contents complement each other perfectly. Constructed in 1930, the building is an architectural masterpiece of the art deco style. The automobiles within it are among the most beautiful ever produced—products of a golden age when luxury and power were the gods of the road. Some 140 classic, antique, special-interest, and one-of-a-kind cars dating from 1898 to the present are on permanent display here.

Indiana was once the automobile capital of the world, and Auburn was its heart, the birthplace of twenty-one of America's early motorcars. The Duesenbergs designed and produced here were the costliest domestic automobiles of the twenties and thirties—commanding prices of $15,000 to $20,000 even in the midst of the Great Depression. Greta Garbo owned one, as did Gary Cooper, Clark Gable, and many of the crowned heads of Europe. They were not only symbols of extravagant wealth, but supremely engineered machines that could hurtle down the highway at speeds up to 130 miles per hour. Today, Duesenbergs are worth hundreds of thousands of dollars as collector cars.

Various models of the Cord, more modest than the Duesenberg but still a cut above the rest, and Auburn are displayed along with more obscure cars, such as the Locomobile, Rauch-Lang, and

McIntyre. A flamboyant 1956 Bentley was owned by the Beatles' John Lennon in the 1960s.

The museum is open daily year-round, except for major winter holidays; from 8:00 A.M. to 6:00 P.M. May through September; 10:00 A.M. to 5:00 P.M. October through April. Admission fee; contact the Auburn-Cord-Dusenberg Museum, 1600 South Wayne Street, Auburn 46706; (219) 925–1444.

Each year on Labor Day weekend, Auburns, Cords, and Duesenbergs from all regions of the United States return to the city of their creation for an annual festival. A highlight of the event is the collector car auction, which has produced many world-record prices. Even for spectators, it's a spectacular show. Write the Auburn-Cord-Duesenberg Festival at the museum's address.

In the tiny town of St. Joe, you can tour the **Ralph Sechler & Son pickle factory,** where multitudes of Midwestern cucumbers are transformed into forty kinds of pickles. Along with the traditional types, the plant produces such unique varieties as candied orange strip and raisin crispy pickles. Free forty-five-minute tours are offered by appointment from 9:00 to 11:00 A.M. and 12:30 to 2:30 P.M. Monday through Friday, May through October. Located at 5686 State Road 1; (219) 337–5461. A salesroom is on the premises.

Delaware County

The winter winds can be fierce in Muncie, the snows deep, and the temperatures subzero, but in a greenhouse on the campus of **Ball State University** a tropical garden of orchids blooms all year long. The Wheeler Orchid Collection contains more varieties of this exquisite flower than any other collection in the world. More than 7,000 plants thrive here, and its species bank was the first such bank anywhere.

The greenhouse is situated in seventeen-acre **Christy Woods,** a mix of arboretum, flower gardens, research facilities, and nature center that serves as an outdoor laboratory for both Ball State students and the general public. Recorded messages guide visitors along trails that wind through the arboretum (tape recorders available at the Orchid House). If you come in April or May, you'll also see a profusion of wildflowers. Free; open 8:00 A.M. to 4:00 P.M. Monday through Saturday year-round; 1:00 to 5:00 P.M. Sunday, April through October. Contact the Department of Biology, (317) 285–8820, 285–8839.

The university's art gallery, located in the Fine Arts Building, houses the Ball/Kraft collection of ancient glass. Free; open 9:00 A.M. to 4:30 P.M. Monday through Friday; 1:30 P.M. to 4:30 P.M. Saturday and Sunday; hours may vary during spring and winter breaks and in the summer; (317) 285–5242.

The name Ball is so prevalent in Muncie because the town is the home of Ball Corporation, the well-known manufacturer of home canning equipment. In addition to the glass food containers that are the company's specialty, Ball Corporation also makes metal and plastic containers, satellites and space systems, and zinc, plastic, and computer-related products. Their museum, located at 345 South High Street, is open to the public from 8:00 A.M. to 4:00 P.M. Monday through Friday; closed holidays; free; (317) 747–6100.

Although small, the Muncie Children's Museum at 306 South Walnut Plaza has been nationally recognized for the hands-on experience it provides. Children can burrow through a human-sized ant farm, learn how to escape from a building "on fire," join a railroad crew laying track across the country, and climb over, under, through, and on ten separate structures. Nominal admission fee; open 10:00 A.M. to 5:00 P.M. Tuesday through Saturday; closed Thanksgiving, December 25, and January 1; (317) 286–1660.

Once the pottery handcrafted by Jim Wishon and Jerry Harrell was sold nationwide in such fine department stores as Nieman-Marcus, Gumps, Burdines, and Carson-Pirie-Scott. Nowadays, their entire output is sold through their showroom at 1508 West Jackson Street in Muncie. You can watch the whole production process, from shaping on the potter's wheel to final firing at a temperature of 2,350 degrees, in the **Wishon-Harrell Pottery Place,** then browse through their showroom of finished stoneware. Standard items include wine carafes, pie plates, pitchers, tea sets, mood lights, and dinnerware. Normally open during daytime hours Monday through Saturday and on Sunday by appointment, but hours vary, and it's best to check in advance by calling (317) 288–6633.

Elkhart County

Some of the best farm cooking you'll ever treat your taste buds to is served up at the Patchwork Quilt Country Inn in Middlebury.

Located on a 260-acre working farm, the dining room is famous for the family-style, all-you-can-eat dinners it serves five nights a week.

When guests arrive, they are served seasonal drinks (no alcohol) in the parlor and encouraged to mingle until the dinner bell sounds. No printed menu—your waitress will give you a choice of foods as each course is served. Everything is offered family style, so you may eat as much as you please. The main entree may be open-hearth baked ham, herb roast beef, burgundy steak, seafood, or buttermilk pecan chicken (the latter once won owner Arletta Lovejoy a $5,000 first prize for the best chicken recipe in the United States). When the dessert tray arrives, you'll find it almost impossible to choose from the luscious-looking treats displayed thereon—if indeed you have enough room left to make any choice at all. You'll be confronted with such unusual meal toppers as Cheddar cheese cake, coffee toffee pie, charlotte russe, walnut torte, fruit parfait, grasshopper pie, and candied violet cake—delectable one and all. Probably at least one dessert will feature strawberries—Ms. Lovejoy's strawberry recipes have also won national fame.

The Patchwork Quilt also offers overnight bed-and-breakfast accommodations every night of the week year-round. Three guest bedrooms are available, each with its own handmade patchwork quilt. A deluxe continental breakfast is included in the room rate of $45 for two; a full country breakfast is available for $2 extra per person.

Middlebury is in the heart of one of the largest Amish settlements in the country, and Ms. Lovejoy offers a guided tour that affords a look at the lifestyle of these people. She also hosts a quilts and crafts tour.

To reach the Patchwork Quilt Inn, go north from Middlebury on State Road 13 for 8 miles to County Road 2, then turn west for about 1 mile to the inn. Dinner is served from 5:00 to 8:00 P.M. Tuesday through Saturday year-round; guests may choose between family-style and plate dinners. Lunch is served from 11:30 A.M. to 2:00 P.M. Tuesday through Saturday, April through October. Prices are moderate; reservations are recommended at all times and are required for dinners from January through March, tours, and overnight accommodations. Closed Sundays, Mondays, and holidays. Write the Patchwork Quilt Inn, 11748 County Road 2, Middlebury 46540; (219) 825–2417.

Carrying on the family tradition is Ms. Lovejoy's daughter, Michele, who with her husband Dick Goebel operates the Open Hearth Bed and Breakfast Inn. Their charming guest house at Echo Valley Farm near Middlebury features three bedrooms and a living room with a fireplace. Outdoors, a gazebo perches at the edge of a duck pond, and paths wander through the woods and fields. Animals are everywhere, both farm and domestic ones. Home-baked rolls and coffee cakes are served at the breakfast table. Accommodations are available Monday through Saturday nights, and rates are similar to those charged at the Patchwork Quilt. To reach Open Hearth, go west from Middlebury on Highway 20 for about 9 miles to State Road 15 and turn north; the entrance road is ¹/₈ mile north of this intersection on the east side of State Road 15. Write Open Hearth Bed and Breakfast, 56782 State Road 15, Echo Valley Farm, Bristol 46507; (219) 848–5256.

You can sample some authentic Amish cuisine, as well as good country cooking, in Middlebury. The Village Inn Restaurant is a small lunchroom whose customers are just as apt to ride up in horse-drawn buggies as in automobiles. All the food is hearty and good—not to mention loaded with calories—but the pies are splendid, prices are quite reasonable, and the people—both staff and guests—are delightful. The Village Inn, located at 104 South Main Street, is open from 5:00 A.M. to 9:00 P.M. Monday through Saturday; (219) 825–2043.

Three miles east of Middlebury on County Road 250N, you can tour the **Deutsch Kase Haus** and watch Amish cheese makers at work. The free samples in the gift shop will help you choose your favorite flavor. Open 8:00 A.M. to 5:00 P.M. Monday through Friday, 8:00 A.M. to 3:00 P.M. Saturday; phone ahead for cheese making schedule at (219) 825–9511.

The area in which Middlebury lies, known as the Crystal Valley, is chock full of fascinating places to explore and enjoy—quilt shops, antique stores, country stores, craft shops, furniture stores, restaurants. For a map of the area and additional information, write the Crystal Valley Tourist Association at P.O. Box 55, Middlebury 46540.

One of the best ways to gain insight into the life-style of the Amish is through a visit to **Amish Acres,** an authentic eighty-acre restoration of a century-old farming community in Nappanee. Amish farmhouses dot the countryside, flat-topped black buggies wander the roads, farmers plow the fields, livestock graze behind split-rail fences, women quilt, dip candles, and bake in an outdoor oven; soapmaking, horseshoeing and meat preservation are demonstrated. Visit a bakery, a meat and cheese shop, an antique soda fountain and fudgery, a cider mill, a smokehouse, a mint still, a sawmill. Life goes on as it did a hundred years ago and as it still does today for the 2,000 Old Order Amish who live in this area.

You may want to take a horse-drawn buggy ride or enjoy the Amish cooking at the Restaurant Barn. The soup is always on in big iron kettles, and such typical dishes as noodles, spiced apples, sweet and sour cabbage salad, and shoofly pie are on the menu.

Amish Acres is located on Highway 6, 1 mile west of Nappanee. The restored farm is open 10:00 A.M. to 7:00 P.M. Monday through Saturday and 11:00 A.M. to 6:00 P.M. Sunday, May through October; tours, rides, and some shops close at 5:00 P.M. The restaurant only is open on April and November weekends; hours vary. Admission fee; special package price for a guided tour. Write the Amish Acres Visitor Information Center, 1600 West Market Street, Nappanee, 46550; (219) 773–4188. The Information Center can also assist you in making reservations for an overnight stay in an area farm home.

Like the Crystal Valley to the northeast, the area in and around Nappanee abounds with interesting shops and Amish businesses that may be toured. The Nappanee Chamber of Commerce, 300 West Lincoln Street, Nappanee 46550 will be happy to provide you with additional information; (219) 773–7812.

Directly north of Nappanee via State Road 19 is the village of Wakarusa, where you can visit the unusual **Bird's-Eye View Museum.** Area buildings of distinctive architectural style are reconstructed from toothpicks, popsicle sticks, and other pint-sized materials—all built on the same scale (1 inch equals 5 feet). It's one of the largest collections of miniatures in the world. Located at 325 South Elkhart Street, it's open evenings and weekends by appointment or chance. Nominal admission fee; (219) 862–4133.

The **Midwest Museum of American Art** would be a gem anywhere, but in the small municipality of Elkhart (population 43,000), it is a crown jewel. Noted for its extensive collections of Norman Rockwell lithographs (believed to be the largest anywhere) and photographs by such distinguished photographers as Ansel Adams, the museum has become one of Indiana's most important art institutions. Nominal admission fee; open 11:00 A.M. to 5:00 P.M. Tuesday through Friday, 1:00 to 4:00 P.M. Saturday and Sunday. Open free of charge 7:00 to 9:00 P.M. Thursday. Located at 429 South Main Street; (219) 293–6660.

Grant County

The death of James Dean on September 30, 1955, catapulted the popular young actor to enduring fame as a cult hero. Although he made only a few movies—*Rebel Without a Cause* and *Giant* among them—Dean gave voice to the restlessness and discontent of his generation through his roles. He died at the age of twenty-four, the victim of a one-car accident on a California highway moments after he had been given a speeding ticket, and his family brought him home to Indiana to bury him. Today, rarely a day goes by—no matter what the weather—that someone doesn't show up in **Park Cemetery** at Fairmount, where Dean grew up, to see his grave and mourn his passing.

For ten years after his death, Warner Brothers received as many as 7,000 letters a month addressed to Dean from devoted fans who refused to accept his death. His tombstone in Park Cemetery, defaced by souvenir seekers, was replaced in 1985. Within a few short months, it too was defaced. A sign that read "This Way to James Dean's Grave" lasted one afternoon, and handfuls of dirt regularly disappear from his burial site. People from as far away as Germany have wanted to purchase a plot here so they can "be buried near Jimmy."

It is a phenomenon that shows no signs of letting up and can never be fully explained—a charisma that reaches out even from the grave. Park Cemetery, open daily dawn to dusk, is on County Road 150E; (317) 948–4040.

The **James Dean/Fairmount Historical Museum** at 203 East Washington Street tells the story of Dean's life through a series of exhibits and displays some of Dean's possessions from a family collection. No admission fee, but donations are accepted. Open 1:00 to 4:00 P.M. Saturday and Sunday, May through October, on February 8 (Dean's birth date), on September 30 (the anniversary of his death), and by appointment. Write Fairmount Historical Museum, Box 92, Fairmount 46928; (317) 948–4555, 948–4776, or 948–5253. Each September, near the date of Dean's death, the museum hosts the Fairmount Museum Days and the James Dean Film Festival. The museum also exhibits memorabilia of Fairmount's other favorite son—Jim Davis, creator of "Garfield the Cat."

The nearby town of Marion, where James Dean was born, is noted for its extraordinary **Easter pageant,** presented each Easter morning at 6:00 A.M. Lauded as the equal of Oberammergau's famous Passion Play, the pageant draws spectators from all fifty states and overseas. Free; for tickets and information, contact the Marion Indiana Easter Pageant, Inc., 118 North Washington Street, Marion 46952; (317) 664-3947.

Ice cream lovers will want to journey over to Upland, home of Taylor University, and visit Ivanhoe's. When they spy the menu here, they'll think they've died and gone to heaven. Sundae and shake flavors are arranged alphabetically—one hundred delicious flavors each, plus a special section for extras. Hoe's, as it's known locally, also serves ice cream sodas, floats, and excellent sandwiches and salads. Located on South Main Street, it's open from 11:00 A.M. to 10:00 P.M. Monday through Thursday; 11:00 A.M. to 11:00 P.M. Friday and Saturday; 2:00 to 10:00 P.M. Sunday; (317) 998-7261.

Howard County

The world has stainless steel because Kokomo inventor Elwood Haynes wanted to please his wife. Well aware of her husband's ingenuity, Ms. Haynes asked him to perfect some tarnish-free dinnerware for her. And in 1912, he did.

The remarkable Mr. Haynes also invented the first successful commercial automobile. On July 4, 1894, he put his gasoline-powered creation to the test on Pumpkinvine Pike east of Kokomo, speeding along at 7 miles per hour for a distance of about 6 miles. That same car is now on display at the Smithsonian Institution in Washington, D.C.

Another of Haynes's inventions is stellite, an alloy used in jet engines, dental instruments, and nuclear power plants. New uses are still being found for it.

The **Elwood Haynes Museum,** housed in Haynes's former residence, contains a vast collection of Haynes's personal possessions and his many inventions. Visitors particularly enjoy the 1905 Haynes automobile, in which the driver sits in the back seat. Other exhibits reflect Howard County's history during and after the area's great gas boom.

The largest natural gas gusher ever brought into production in this country was struck in what is now southeast Kokomo in 1887. Almost overnight the town was transformed into a center of industry. Kokomo's many contributions to the industrial growth of America, in addition to Haynes's inventions, have earned it the nickname, "City of Firsts." Among the items first produced here were the pneumatic rubber tire, carburetor, mechanical corn picker, canned tomato juice, and the all-transistor car radio. All these and more are featured in the upstairs rooms of the Elwood Haynes Museum, located at 1915 South Webster Street. Free of charge, it's open from 1:00 to 4:00 P.M. Tuesday through Saturday, 1:00 to 5:00 P.M. Sunday; closed Mondays and holidays; (317) 452–3471.

Just to the northwest of the Haynes Museum, at 902 West Deffenbaugh Street, enter Highland Park and view Kokomo's own Big Ben. Ben was a crossbred Hereford steer who at the time of his birth in 1902 was proclaimed to be the largest calf in the world. When you see Ben, you won't find it hard to believe. At four years of age, the steer weighed 4,720 pounds, stood 6 feet 4 inches tall, measured 13 feet 6 inches in girth, and was an astonishing 16 feet 8 inches long from his nose to the tip of his tail. For many years, he was exhibited around the country in circuses and side shows. He had to be destroyed in 1911 after breaking his leg, and shortly thereafter, he was stuffed. Today, he occupies a place of honor in a glass-enclosed building in the park.

Another of Kokomo's giant wonders is preserved just across the road from Ben. Resting on a concrete base and enclosed by a cast-iron fence is the stump of a huge sycamore tree. The stump—12 feet tall and 51 feet in circumference—is impressive enough, but it only hints at the magnificent tree of which it once was a part. Originally more than 100 feet in height, the tree grew to maturity on a farm west of Kokomo. Its hollow trunk once housed a telephone booth large enough to accommodate a dozen people at a time. When the tree was storm-damaged around 1915, the enormous stump was pulled to its present location by a house mover.

The **Kokomo Opalescent Glass Co.,** in operation since 1888, once supplied glass to Louis C. Tiffany. Today, this small factory is known worldwide as a leading producer of fine art glass, and visitors can watch the glass-making process from beginning to end. Free tours Monday through Friday, except in December; call for times. An adjoining retail shop is open 9:00 A.M. to 5:00 P.M. Monday through Saturday. Located at 1310 South Market Street; (317) 457–1829.

Kosciusko County

Some towns will do almost anything to get attention. Mentone grabbed its share of publicity by erecting a monument unique in the world. There it stands, right next to Main Street—a 12-foot-high, 3,000-pound **concrete egg.** If, when in Mentone, anyone should ask the perennial puzzler, "Which came first, the chicken or the egg?" the answer would almost certainly have to be "the egg." Pity the poor chicken who would have to handle this one!

In 1946, when the monument was first "laid," every farmer in the area had a chicken house, and eggs were shipped all over the Midwest. That enterprise declined in the 1950s, but the lives of the town's 950 residents are still intertwined with eggs and chickens today. Local businesses hatch eggs, provide chicken meat for soup companies, and separate egg whites from the yolks for bakeries. And each June, the community celebrates industry, heritage, and monument with an egg festival. Contact the Mentone Chamber of Commerce, Box 366, Mentone 46539; (219) 353–7933.

Next to the city park on State Road 25 West in Mentone, you'll find the **Lawrence D. Bell Aircraft Museum.** It contains the memorabilia of Larry Bell, the Mentone native who forsook eggs and instead founded the Bell Aircraft Corporation. Bell produced twenty aviation firsts, including the world's first commercial helicopter and the nation's first jet-propelled airplane. Scale models of many Bell aircraft are on display. Guided tours are offered from 1:00 to 5:00 P.M. Sunday from June through August; other times by appointment. Nominal admission fee; contact the Museum at Box 411, Mentone 46539; (219) 353–7228, 353–7647.

In honor of Kosciusko County's agricultural heritage, the Greater Warsaw Area Chamber of Commerce has put together two drive-yourself farm tours. Scenic country roads lead visitors by farms that produce spearmint, chickens, buffalo, pigs, sheep, cattle, and various fruits and vegetables. Maple Leaf Farms is the largest producer of ducklings in the the country and maybe the world. Ault Stables trains harness horses. Many facilities offer guided tours by prearrangement. For free maps, contact the Chamber of Commerce at 313 South Buffalo Street, Warsaw 46580; (219) 267–6311.

Lagrange County

No place in America has done better by its junk than the tiny hamlet of Shipshewana. Each Tuesday and Wednesday from May through October, it puts on what may be the biggest small-town sale in the country. It's almost certain that anything you've ever wanted has at one time or another been available at the **Shipshewana** (Shipshe for short) **Auction and Flea Market.** The items available at one recent sale included old beer cans, garden tools, round oak tables, new hats and clothing at discount prices, door knobs, bubble gum machines, rare books, antique china, long-legged underwear, fenceposts, Aladdin lamps, fishing rods, parts for old wagons, extra pieces for a Lionel train set, hand and power tools, quilts, a worn-out butter churn, a half-full can of green house paint, baseball cards, some homemade toy alligators, and, perhaps the most unusual item ever offered here, a used tombstone.

Wednesday is the biggest business day. In addition to the flea market, held over from Tuesday, there's a livestock sale and miscellaneous auction. The vast array of sale items keeps about a dozen auctioneers busy from 7:00 A.M. on throughout the afternoon, while in the livestock barn farmers do some hot and heavy bidding on 2,500 head of cattle, sheep, and pigs. Outside, in the flea market yard, nearly 1,000 vendors display their wares. On an average Wednesday, $200,000 worth of livestock and goods changes hands, not including the several thousand dollars spent at the flea market. Although it would be a compliment to describe some of the merchandise as junk, there are also many valuable antiques and hard-to-find items.

The Shipshe Auction hosts as many as 30,000 visitors a day. License plates reveal they come from every state in the Union and Canada. When winter comes, the flea market closes down, but the Wednesday auction simply moves under cover and continues throughout the year.

Each Friday, the auction yard is the scene of a horse auction that draws buyers and sellers from all over North America to deal in Amish draft horses, reputed to be some of the finest in the land. (Shipshewana sits right in the heart of one of the largest Amish settlements in the United States.)

You'll have a grand time at the Shipshe Auction even if you

don't buy a thing. It's one of the world's great spectator events. The auction yards are located on State Road 5 at the south edge of Shipshewana. For more details, write the Shipshewana Auction and Flea Market, Box 185, Shipshewana 46565; (219) 768–4129.

Since all the people who attend Shipshe's various auctions have to eat, there's a special Auction Restaurant operated from one of the sale barns that's open just two days a week. It dishes up delicious Amish food nonstop from 5:00 A.M. to 7:30 P.M. Tuesday and from 5:00 A.M. until the sales close for the day on Wednesday; (219) 768–4129.

Another fine Amish meal can be had at the Buggy Wheel Restaurant on Morton Street in downtown Shipshewana. Some of the more unusual breakfast fare includes mush, headcheese, and, on Thursday only, tomato gravy, but there are plenty of eggs, bacon, and potatoes on hand, too. All lunches are served cafeteria-style, while a soup, salad, and dessert buffet is a specialty on Friday and Saturday evenings. All meals are not offered every day; open 5:00 A.M. to 7:00 P.M. Monday through Thursday, 5:00 A.M. to 8:00 P.M. Friday and Saturday, May through October; winter hours vary; (219) 768–4444.

To learn more about the Mennonite/Amish life-style and heritage, explore the exhibits at the recently opened **Menno-Hof Visitors Center** on State Road 5 South opposite the Shipshewana Auction grounds. You'll also find information about the area's many Amish-related businesses and attractions. Hours vary; call (219) 768–4117.

Stretching along the Pigeon River in northeastern Lagrange County and reaching eastward into Steuben County, is the 11,500-acre Pigeon River State Fish and Wildlife Area. The hauntingly beautiful stream, edged by lush vegetation, choked with hyacinths, flows through an outstanding variety of habitats—marshes, meadows, woods, swamps, and bogs. Birdwatchers love this area; some 216 species of birds, many of them rare, have been sighted here. In the spring and early summer, wildflowers run rampant. It's all reminiscent of the Southland's fabled Suwannee River—a fine and private place in which to study nature, canoe, hunt mushrooms, nuts and berries; hike, fish, pitch a tent, or ski cross-country.

The **Tamarack Bog State Nature Preserve** near the center of the wildlife area contains the largest tamarack swamp in Indiana and harbors such unique plants as the insectivorous pitcher plant and sundew. Contact the Pigeon River State Fish and Wildlife Area, Box 71, Mongo 46771; (219) 367–2164.

Miami County

The circus first came to Peru, Indiana, in the late 1800s, and it remains there to this day, the single most dominant force in the community.

It all began with native son Ben Wallace, who owned a livery stable in Peru. One winter a broken-down animal show limped into town and found shelter in Ben's stable. When spring came, Ben was left with all the animals in lieu of a fee. Using his Hoosier ingenuity, Ben spiffed things up a bit, started his own circus, and built it into one of the world's finest—the Hagenbeck-Wallace Circus. Winter quarters were set up on the vast farm fields just outside of town, and other major circuses of the day, lured by the excellent facilities, also came to Peru in the off-season.

Among the show business greats who spent at least part of the year here were Clyde Beatty, the noted animal trainer (like Ben Wallace, a native son); Emmett Kelly, the renowned clown; Willi Wilno, "the human cannonball"; and Tom Mix, who later starred in Hollywood westerns. Red Skelton left his home in southern Indiana when he was just a boy to join the Hagenbeck-Wallace Circus and to launch one of the most famous and enduring careers in the entertainment business.

The circus and Peru with it flourished for many years before passing into near oblivion, but local folks, many of them direct descendants of stars who brightened the firmament of circus history, decided that their town's unique heritage should be preserved forever. And so, each year in the third week of July, the circus once again comes to Peru.

The performers, who must be residents of Miami County, range in age from six to early twenties, and they are so skillful, you'll find it difficult to believe that this is not a professional show. Since the children of Peru are to the circus born—beginning their training in earliest childhood under the tutelage of some of the finest circus pros in the country—a constant supply of new talent is available. All the components of the old-time circus are here—aerialists, clowns, tightrope walkers, human pyramids, gymnasts, animal trainers, and much more. The whole thing is so authentic and entertaining that NBC Television once filmed an hour-long documentary about it.

There are several performances during the annual festival, as well as a giant parade complete with calliopes, old circus wagons, and the rousing music of the Circus City Band. For additional information, contact the Circus City Festival Office, Broadway at Seventh, Peru 46970; (317) 472–3918.

The town's **Circus City Museum,** located in the Festival Office at 154 North Broadway, contains one of the finest collections of circus relics in the world and sells circus souvenirs in an unusual gift shop. It's open free of charge 9:00 A.M. to noon and 1:00 to 5:00 P.M. Monday through Saturday, April through October; closed holidays. During festival week, hours are extended.

In 1985, the city obtained an array of circus memorabilia from the now-defunct Circus Hall of Fame at Sarasota, Florida, and plans are afoot to reestablish the hall of fame locally. The collection, currently housed in various places throughout the community, includes such rarities as an 1892 calliope with thirty-two steam-operated whistles and an 11-foot-tall wagon built to haul giraffes.

Even in death, Ben Wallace chose to remain in Peru. He is buried in **Mount Hope Cemetery** on 12th Street along with another well-known native son, Cole Porter. One of the few songwriters who wrote both words and music, Porter penned such classics as "Night and Day," "When They Begin the Beguine," "I've Got You Under My Skin," and "What Is This Thing Called Love?" The Miami County Historical Society—(317) 472–3901, extension 40—can direct you to his birthplace, his mother's home, and his grandmother's home. None are open to the public, but they can be seen from the road.

Grissom Air Force Base, located just southwest of the junction of Highway 31 and State Road 218 a few miles south of Peru, has an outdoor museum of early aircraft that will appeal to aviation buffs. Among the planes you'll see is Passionate Paulette, the B-25 bomber that appeared in the movie *Catch 22.* Grissom is the home of the 305th Air Refueling Wing of the Strategic Air Command, whose crews are responsible for the performance of high-speed, jet-to-jet aerial refueling.

Drop in anytime to see the aircraft museum, but the rest of the base can be visited only via a free guided tour. Because of security reasons, tours must be arranged at least thirty days in advance. Only groups of fifteen or more are scheduled, but it may be possible for you to join an existing tour. Minimum age is seven. You'll be able to inspect a KC-135 refueling aircraft (often called the Air Force version of the Boeing 707) and visit any shop in which your group is interested except those in the classified area. Contact Public Affairs Office, 305 AREFW, Grissom Air Force Base 46971; (317) 689-2104.

Randolph County

At the **Silver Towne Coin Shop** in Winchester, all that glitters is gold—or silver—and the beautiful antique-decorated showrooms in which the collections are displayed are as dazzling as the shop's wares. Open 8:00 A.M. to 5:00 P.M. Monday through Friday. Located just west of Highway 27 on the north side of Union Street; (317) 584-7481.

People from all over the world flock to Winchester each July to attend the **International Hawaiian Steel Guitar Convention.** For three days, the air is filled with music, and on Saturday night, everyone's invited to a luau. Contact Charles Moore, RR 1, Winchester 47394, (317) 584-6746, or the Winchester Chamber of Commerce, 213½ South Main Street, Winchester 47394; (317) 584-3731.

Steuben County

Majestic Potawatomi Inn, the only state park inn in northern Indiana, is one of the finest in the system. Resembling an Old English lodge, it sits in a clearing on the shore of Lake James in 1,200-acre **Pokagon State Park** near Angola.

Winter is king here, and the main treat is a refrigerated toboggan slide, generally open from Thanksgiving Day through February, that whisks you over the hills and through the woods at 35–40 miles per hour. In this snowy park tucked into the northeastern corner of the Hoosier State, winter visitors will also find an ice-skating pond, a sledding hill, and cross-country ski trails. Toboggans and cross-country ski equipment can be rented in the park.

After frolicking in the chilly outdoors all day, retire to the inn for a sauna and whirlpool bath, do a few laps in the indoor pool, or bask in the warmth of the red brick fireplace.

The inn features more than eighty rooms, including some nearby sleeping cabins, and serves three meals daily in its highly rated dining room. Roast beef is a daily feature on a dinner menu that usually includes a choice of a seafood, steak, and chicken or ham dish. The rates are hard to beat—from $31–$36 a night for a double room and from $2.50–$8.50 for dinner, with lunch and breakfast rates even cheaper.

Although Pokagon State Park and its inn have gained a reputation as a winter resort, people also come here in other seasons, when the forests and the sweeping lawns of the inn are a lush green, park lakes are ice-free for swimmers and fishermen, and park trails accommodate hikers instead of skiers. Horses may be rented at the saddle barn, and the tennis and basketball courts see some heavy use.

The Nature Center is popular year-round, with naturalists always on hand to interpret each of Nature's moods. Bison and elk reside in nearby pens. One park trail leads to the marshes, swamps, and forests of the **Potawatomi State Nature Preserve.** The largest known tamarack and yellow birch trees in the state, the only northern white cedars known to exist in Indiana, and several species of wild orchids grow within the preserve's 208 acres.

For information about either the park or the inn, write Pokagon State Park, Route 2, Box 129, Angola 46703; the park phone is (219) 833–2012, the inn (219) 833–1077. To reach the park, go west from Angola on Highway 20 to Interstate 69. Turn north onto Interstate 69 and proceed to State Road 727; State Road 727 leads west from Interstate 69 to the park entrance.

All of Steuben County is noted for its natural beauty. Its combination of 101 lakes and verdant forests have earned it the nickname, "Switzerland of Indiana," and no less an impressario than P. T. Barnum once pronounced Lake James "the most beautiful body of water I have ever seen!" What's more, Steuben County contains six state nature preserves, more than any other county in the state; you can learn more about them by contacting the Department of Natural Resources, Division of Nature Preserves, State Office Building, Indianapolis 46204; (317) 232–4052.

Off the Beaten Path in Northwest Indiana

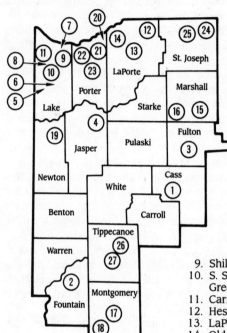

9. Shilo Arabian Farms, Inc.
10. S. S. Constantine and Helen
    Greek Orthodox Cathedral
11. Carmelite Shrines
12. Hesston Gardens
13. LaPorte County Museum
14. Old Lighthouse Museum
15. Antique Motorcycle Museum
16. Black Horse Troop
17. Old Jail Museum
18. Shades State Park
19. Ponderosa Sun Club
20. House of Tomorrow
21. Dunes State Park
22. Indiana Dunes National
    Lakeshore
23. Wilbur H. Cummings
    Museum of Electronics
24. 100 Center Complex
25. Martin Blad Mint Farm
26. Wolf Park
27. Clegg Memorial Garden

1. France Park
2. Portland Arch
3. Round Barn Festival
4. Jasper-Pulaski State Fish and
   Wildlife Area
5. German Methodist Cemetery
   Prairie
6. Grand Old Lady of Lake
   County
   Lake County Jail
7. El-Amin Mosque
8. Grand Trunk Depot Museum

Northwest Indiana

Cass County

The pride of Logansport is its turn-of-the-century carousel. Now more than eighty years old, it is one of the only two all-wood, hand-carved merry-go-rounds still operating in Indiana (the other is in the Indianapolis Children's Museum). Delighted riders compete for a mount on the outer side and the chance to snag the coveted brass ring as the carousel spins round and round. Their brightly colored steeds—a mix of thirty-one horses, three goats, three reindeer, three giraffes, a lion, and a tiger—were produced by the talented hands of German craftsman Gustav A. Dentzel, who moved to the United States in 1860 and became this country's chief carousel maker.

Although the carousel is owned by a nonprofit citizens' group, a small fee is charged for each ride to help offset the cost of maintenance. You'll find the merry-go-round in Riverside City Park at 1300 Riverside Drive—just follow the sound of music. It operates daily from Memorial Day through Labor Day, but hours may vary. Contact Eric Wolf, Box 388, Logansport 46947; (219) 753–6161.

Four miles west of Logansport off Highway 24, you'll come upon **France Park** and its picturesque swimming hole. An abandoned stone quarry, partially hemmed in by precipitous cliffs, is filled with clear, brisk water that's irresistible on a hot summer day. Scuba and cliff divers like it, too.

Patches of woodland and a mossy, 15-foot waterfall on Paw Paw Creek add touches of beauty to the 500-acre county park. Visitors will also find a water slide, more than 800 campsites, and, near the entrance, a century-old log cabin. Nominal admission fee; open daily year-round. Write France Park, RR 6, Logansport 46947; (219) 753–2928.

Fountain County

It will never give the folks in Utah anything to worry about, but Indiana does have a stone arch that's so unique it's been declared both a National Natural Landmark and a state nature preserve.

Through the years, the meanderings of a tiny stream in north-western Fountain County have carved a 30-foot by 12-foot opening through a massive sandstone formation and created a natural bridge known as **Portland Arch.** Nearby, Bear Creek flows through a deep ravine edged by rugged sandstone cliffs. The rare bush honeysuckle grows here, and this is the only known site in the state where the Canada blueberry is found. At times, a cover of mosses and lichens and several species of ferns growing in the crevices of the cliffs create a landscape of green velvet. A quaint pioneer cemetery on the 253-acre preserve contains eleven marked graves.

Portland Arch State Nature Preserve is located on the south side of the town of Fountain. Signs lead the way to the preserve and two parking lots, each adjoined by a self-guiding trail. The loop trail leading from the first and main parking lot follows a hilly route about 1 mile long to Portland Arch. For additional information, contact Department of Natural Resources, Division of Nature Preserves, 605-B State Office Bldg., Indianapolis 46204; (317) 232–4052.

Fulton County

Fulton County is peppered with round barns, the legacy of a turn-of-the-century fad. At last count, nine were still standing, the last of which was built in 1924. The main idea behind this flurry of round-barn building was to create one centralized feeding station for livestock, thus increasing the efficiency of the farmer's operation. The barns proved to be impractical to heat and light in those days, however, and the idea was abandoned. Officially, the barns are not open to the public, but the local Round Barn Association will provide you with a free map that shows the location of each one. Many owners are happy to show you through their barns if they're at home when you arrive, and several barns are open to the public during the second weekend of each July when the county celebrates a **Round Barn Festival.** The existing barns are kept in excellent repair, and they are both unusual and beautiful to behold. No two are alike.

Write the Fulton County Round Barn Association, P.O. Box 512, Rochester 46975; (219) 223–5329.

Jasper County

Each fall, one of Indiana's most magnificent natural spectacles takes place at the 8,000-acre **Jasper-Pulaski State Fish and Wildlife Area.** During the last week in October and the first week in November, some 12,000 greater sandhill cranes pause here to rest on their annual journey south for the winter. Jasper-Pulaski is believed to be the only place east of the Mississippi River where this unusual species stops en masse during migration.

These beautiful blue-gray birds, which stand about 3½ feet tall and have a wing span of up to 7 feet, are as impressive to hear as they are to look at. The best times to view them are at dawn, when they rise up from the misty marshes and call to each other in noisy unison, and again at sunset, when they return to the marsh for the night.

You can pick up some literature about the cranes and a free observation permit at the area headquarters, then continue on to one of two observation towers.

The cranes also migrate through Jasper-Pulaski in the spring, between late February and mid-April, but are usually present in greater concentration in the fall.

Although the sandhills are the main attraction, other wildlife species are here as well. Canada geese, quail, woodcock, and deer live in the wild year-round, and some elk and bison roam fenced-in pastures. Part of Jasper-Pulaski serves as a game farm where pheasant are reared as stock for fish and wildlife areas throughout the state. Natural history and wildlife exhibits are maintained in one of the service buildings, and hiking trails wind through the area.

Located in the area's northwest corner is the 480-acre Tefft Savanna State Nature Preserve, home to many plants that are extremely rare in the Midwest. The entire fish and wildlife area actually occupies parts of three counties—Jasper, Pulaski, and Starke—but the majority of its 8,000 acres are in Jasper County. It's open daily, year-round, at all times, and entrance is free. The headquarters office is open 7:00 A.M. to 3:30 P.M. Monday through Friday, but hours may be extended in certain seasons.

To reach the refuge, go west from Highway 421 in northwestern Pulaski County on State Road 143 for 1½ miles to the entrance on the right side of the road; follow the signs. Write

Jasper-Pulaski State Fish and Wildlife Area, RR 1, Box 166, Medaryville 47957; (219) 843–4841.

Lake County

When the first white settlers came to Indiana, seven-eighths of the land was covered with a forest so dense that a squirrel could visit every tree in the state without ever once touching the ground. The far northwest corner, including what is now Lake County, was a sea of grass—grass so tall in places that a man on horseback could not be seen above it. It was a long time before man realized the value of saving some remnants of that original landscape, and by then most of it was irretrievably gone.

Two of the finest examples still in existence can be seen in Lake County. **German Methodist Cemetery Prairie** covers just one acre at the rear of the cemetery for which it's named, but more than eighty rare and vanishing plant species thrive in its rich black soil. In late summer, when most of them are in bloom, it is a place of incredible beauty.

This tiny preserve is probably the most botanically diverse acre in Indiana. You'll find it in the midst of some farm fields on the east side of Highway 41, 1 mile south of the intersection of Highway 41 and 141st Street in Cedar Lake. The old cemetery is still there and should be respected. Behind it is the prairie, surrounded by a chain-link fence to protect the fragile plant life. For additional information, contact The Nature Conservancy, Indiana Field Office, 4200 North Michigan Street, Indianapolis 46208; (317) 923–7547.

Hoosier Prairie sprawls over 439 acres near Griffith and offers some 300 species of native plants. Some of its grasses reach 12 feet in height. A trail about 2 miles long leads through some of the preserve's less sensitive areas and permits a look at the diverse habitats. You may even spot a deer along the way. Hoosier Prairie is located west of Griffith on the south side of Main Street; a small parking lot is near the trailhead. Open daily, year-round, during daylight hours; free. Write the Department of Natural Resources, Division of Nature Preserves, 605-B State Office Building, Indianapolis 46204; (317) 232–4052.

At Griffith, an active railroad center at the turn of the century, you can visit a renovated train station known as the **Grand**

Trunk Depot Museum and inspect such railroad memorabilia as telegraph equipment, an instrument panel, model trains, a watchman's hut, and a C&O one-cylinder motorcar used for track inspection. Free; located at 201 South Broad Street; open 2:00 to 4:00 P.M. Sunday; (219) 924–7500 or 924–2155.

The **Carmelite Shrines** in Munster offer a haven of serenity. On the grounds are twenty shrines that display Italian sculptures in a grotto studded with crystals and unusual rocks. The overall effect is enhanced by special lighting. You'll also find an arboretum and, in the monastery, a replica of the Vatican's Private Audience Hall. Grounds open free of charge from 1:00 to 5:00 P.M. daily, weather permitting; building interiors can usually be seen upon request. The shrines are located at 1628 Ridge Road, ¹/₂ mile west of Highway 41; (219) 838–5050 or 838–7111.

If antiquing is high on your list of priorities, you'll want to sample the shops of Lowell, where a cluster of ten stores offers quite a mix of antiques and collectibles. Contact the Lowell Chamber of Commerce, P.O. Box 303, Lowell 46356; (219) 696–0231, for more information.

When hunger pangs strike, head for Teibel's Restaurant in Schererville. Teibel's first opened its doors in 1929, the year the stock market crashed and launched the Great Depression. The fact that the restaurant operated continuously through all those lean years and still thrives today should tell you something. One of those is that the old family recipe for fried chicken, which initially earned the restaurant its reputation, is a winner. The chicken (as well as fried perch) is served on an all-you-can-eat basis. Prices are moderate. Open 11:00 A.M. to 10:00 P.M. Sunday through Thursday, 11:00 A.M. to 11:00 P.M. Friday and Saturday. Located at the corner of Highway 41 and Highway 30; (219) 865–2000.

Many people think Arabians are the most beautiful of all horses. At Hobart, you can tour the world's largest Arabian horse farm and decide for yourself. Contact **Shilo Arabian Farms, Inc.,** 6900 Ainsworth Road; (219) 947–2507.

Crown Point is dominated by the **"Grand Old Lady of Lake County,"** the magnificent old courthouse that many regard as Indiana's most impressive. Built in 1878, it served as the seat of county government until 1974. Today it houses more than twenty craft and specialty shops, including a fascinating puzzle shop and the Women's Exchange Resale Shop (profits aid courthouse restoration), as well as the Lake County Historical Museum. Don't miss its arched brick ceilings and intriguing hallways. The courthouse is located at the corner of Joliet and Court streets; its shops are generally open from 10:00 A.M. to 5:00 P.M. Monday through Thursday and Saturday; 10:00 A.M. to 8:00 P.M. on Friday; (219) 663–0660. Museum open noon to 4:00 P.M. Friday through Sunday, spring through fall; other times by appointment. Nominal admission fee; (219) 663–2765 or 663–2866.

In 1896, William Jennings Bryan stood on the courthouse steps and campaigned for the presidency. A then unknown car designer, Louis Chevrolet, came here to accept the winner's cup for the first major auto race in the United States, a race held in 1909 that was the forerunner of the Indy 500. From 1916 to 1941, the courthouse became famous for its instant marriages; the usual blood test and three-day waiting period were not required here. Among the thousands married at the courthouse during that period were Joe DiMaggio, Red Grange, Colleen Moore, Tom Mix, Ronald Reagan, and, at the height of his career, Rudolph Valentino.

Perhaps all of these events are overshadowed in history, though, by a 1934 happening that brought national notoriety to Crown Point. John Dillinger, the famous bank robber who was then the nation's most wanted criminal, had been captured in Tucson, Arizona, and returned to the **Lake County Jail** near the courthouse to await trial. Even though it was considered the most escape-proof facility of its time, the jail nevertheless was surrounded by police and national guardsmen for additional security. The irrepressible Mr. Dillinger, never one to take things lying down, carved himself a gun from a wooden washboard, painted it black with shoe polish, and promptly made his escape in the sheriff's car. Although the type of car is not noted in most accounts of the incident, it was probably a Ford. Dillinger was known to favor Fords and once wrote a personal letter to Henry Ford to thank him for building "such wonderful cars." The dark, dank jail cell where Dillinger was held can still be seen. Contact the Crown Point Chamber of Commerce, P.O. Box 343, Crown Point 46307; (219) 663–1800.

Close by is J.D.'s Speakeasy, a restaurant with a 1930s motif and a Dillinger museum that includes his gruesome death mask and bulletproof vest. Enter by giving the password, "Sons of the Boss," and be seated in a booth enclosed by steel jail bars. The fun-to-read menu continues the theme with Bugs Moran burgers and desserts that are Public Enemies Number One through Six.

Located at 211 South East Street; open 11:00 A.M. to 10:00 P.M. Monday through Saturday, noon to 8:00 P.M. Sunday; (219) 663–8242.

The magnificent **SS. Constantine and Helen Greek Orthodox Cathedral** rises from amidst thirty-seven acres of grounds at 8000 Madison Street in Merrillville. The only one in the state, it features twenty-five large stained-glass windows, Byzantine mosaic work, and a rotunda 100 feet in diameter and 50 feet high. Open 9:00 A.M. to 5:00 P.M. Monday through Friday, 10:00 A.M. to 2:00 P.M. Saturday. Each year, on the second weekend of July, a Grecian festival takes place here; (219) 769–2481.

Until recently, the city of Gary was known as Steeltown, U.S.A., but it is perhaps better known now as the birthplace of the phenomenon of the eighties. Throughout the city, billboards proclaim that Michael Jackson is "Another Great Gary Product," as well as the "World's Number One Entertainer." Michael was born here in August 1958 and grew up in a small, two-bedroom house located at 2300 Jackson Street (named long ago in honor of President Andrew Jackson). Although it's not open to the public, the house can be viewed from the street. Don't be surprised, though, if you get lost in the crowd—a steady stream of fans passes by daily. Many folks hereabout still remember the Jackson Five's first public appearance on the stage of Gary's Roosevelt High School in 1965. Shy Michael had to be dragged onto the stage, but what happened from that moment on is show business history.

While in Gary, you may also want to visit the **El-Amin Mosque** at 3702 West 11th Street. One of the largest mosques in the United States, it serves the area's Lebanese, Arabs, Turks, and Egyptians and is architecturally interesting; (219) 949–1854.

The frog legs served at Phil Smidt & Son in Hammond have been celebrated for all of the more than seventy-five years that the restaurant has been in business. Once they were gathered from the shore of nearby Lake Michigan; today, like all frog legs served in restaurants in the United States, they come from Bangladesh. They are still delicious, however, and what's more, they're served in a stunning room. One side is open; two walls are a soft rose hue; the third bears murals of gigantic roses, done in high-gloss paint on a shiny black background. Soft light filters through blocks of aquarium glass. The white tablecloths are bordered in pink, and each place is set with rose-colored napkins and rose-embossed water glasses. Be sure to ask to be seated in the Rose Room; there are five other dining rooms as well.

Another specialty of the house is lake perch, served whole or boned and cooked to perfection. Top off your meal with warm gooseberry pie.

Outside, freight trains rumble by, and smokestacks spew smoke—an incredible contrast to the beauty within.

You'll find Phil Smidt & Son at 1205 North Calumet Avenue; it's open for lunch and dinner from 11:15 A.M. to 9:30 P.M., Monday through Thursday; 11:15 A.M. to 10:30 P.M. Friday and Saturday; (219) 659–0025.

LaPorte County

The tiny town of Hesston is nestled in the midst of some of the prettiest scenery in dunes country. It was here, some fifty years ago, that Father Joseph G. Sokolowski planted the flowers and trees and shrubs that grew into the beautiful gardens you see today. At first appearance, the **Hesston Gardens** resemble a wild woodland, as though created by Nature alone. But as you wander along narrow, winding paths, you'll realize how well kept and well planned the gardens really are. Father Sokolowski, a Greek Orthodox priest, nurtures his gardens as a labor of love and happily shares them with all visitors. Each Sunday at 10:00 A.M., he holds Mass in a tiny chapel in the woods that is filled with paintings and icons. He also maintains part of his residence as a museum of religious artifacts. To support his avocation, he sells antiques. Visitors are welcome daily, from dawn to dusk, May through October. The best time to see the gardens is in May and June, when hundreds of azaleas and rhododendrons are in bloom. There is no admission charge, but donations are gratefully accepted. To reach the gardens, go north from the town of La-Porte on State Road 39. Just before you reach the Michigan border, turn east on County Road 1000N. Continue east to County Road 215E and turn north for about one-eighth mile. The entrance road, shrouded in trees, is on the west side of 215E. Contact Father Sokolowski at 10254 North 215 East, LaPorte 46350; (219) 778–2421.

Back on 1000N, you can see the Hesston Steam Museum. Spread out over a 155-acre site is an assemblage of steam-powered equipment worth several million dollars—trains, cranes, buzz saws, and a boat among them. You can take a 2-mile ride on a steam railroad or watch a miniature railroad, authentic to the tiniest detail, whiz by on a 3½-inch track. Feel free to toot a horn or ring a bell—it's that type of place.

You can walk through the exhibit any day except Monday, but the equipment is in operation 1:00 to 6:00 P.M. on Saturday, Sunday, and holidays, Memorial Day weekend through Labor Day, and Sunday only from Labor Day through October. An especially exuberant celebration takes place during the Annual Labor Day Weekend Steam Show. The outdoor museum is located on the north side of County Road 1000N, approximately 2½ miles east of State Road 39; a nominal fee is charged for train rides. Contact the Steam Society at 2940 Mt. Claire Way, Long Beach, Michigan City 46360; (219) 872–7405 or 872–5055.

In the town of LaPorte, you can take a free tour of the **LaPorte County Museum.** The more than 20,000 items on exhibit include the W. A. Jones collection of antique firearms and weapons, which is recognized as the best of its kind in the United States and one of the three best in the world.

There's also a folklore display that tells the story of Belle Gunness, LaPorte's Madam Bluebeard, who, in the early 1900s, lured at least a dozen men to her farm north of town by promising to marry them. Once there, the would-be husbands were promptly killed for their money and buried in the farmyard. The museum, located in the new courthouse adjacent to Independence Square, is open free of charge from 10:00 A.M. to 4:30 P.M., Monday through Friday, and from 1:00 to 4:00 P.M. on the first Sunday of each month (closed holidays); (219) 326–6808.

At the Angelo Bernacchi Greenhouses, you can treat your visual and olfactory senses to the thousands of growing green things that make this the largest grower and retailer of plants in the entire Midwest. There are acres to browse through all year long. The retail shop is open 9:00 A.M. to 5:00 P.M. Monday through Saturday; special tours on May 1 and December 1. Located at 1010 Fox Street, LaPorte; (219) 362–6202.

The Barker Civic Center at 631 Washington Street in Michigan City exudes turn-of-the-century elegance. Once the home of millionaire industrialist John H. Barker, it contains thirty-eight rooms, ten bathrooms, several fireplaces with hand-carved teak, walnut, or mahogany woodwork and a mirrored ballroom. Adjacent to the library terrace is a sunken Italian garden. Tours at 10:00 A.M., 11:30 A.M., and 1:00 P.M. Monday through Friday, year-round; also at noon and 2:00 P.M. Saturday and Sunday, June through October; closed major holidays. Admission fee; (219) 873–1520.

Not far away, a fishing pier that extends into Lake Michigan offers a view of Indiana's only operating lighthouse. On a clear day, you can also see the Chicago skyline.

The area's nautical history is explored at the **Old Lighthouse Museum** in Washington Park, Michigan City's ninety-acre lake-front park. Situated on Heisman Harbor Road at the park's west entrance, the museum contains a rare 4th Order Fresnel lens, shipbuilding tools and other maritime artifacts. Open 1:00 to 4:00 P.M. Tuesday through Sunday, year-round; closed Mondays and holidays. Nominal admission charge; (219) 872–6133 or 872–3273.

Washington Park's zoo features more than 180 species of animals and raises more Bengal tigers than any zoo in the United States. Within its boundaries, an observation tower atop a dune offers some spectacular bird's-eye views. The zoo is open daily 10:30 A.M. to 6:00 P.M., Memorial Day through Labor Day; 10:30 A.M. to 3:00 P.M. daily the rest of the year; small admission fee; (219) 873–1510.

Marshall County

Larry Feece started collecting motorcyles in 1960, when he was just a teenager. Today, he owns approximately 300 bikes, a sizable collection that over the years outgrew both his house and his wife's patience. So Larry developed the **Antique Motorcycle Museum,** believed to be the only museum in the country devoted entirely to motorcycles. At any given time, about half of the still-growing collection, which includes an 1899 Peugeot (Larry's oldest bike), an original Johnson Motorbike, and a 1934 James brought over from England, is on display. Open 9:00 A.M. to 5:00 P.M. Saturday and Sunday, April through October; nominal admission fee. Located at 139 East Walnut Street in Argos; (219) 892–5177 (museum) or (219) 935–2477 (twenty-four-hour answering service).

Since the U.S. Army Cavalry was disbanded in 1950, the **Black Horse Troop** of Culver Military Academy (a college preparatory boarding school) has been the nation's largest mounted military organization. The 144 young men who comprise its ranks hone their skills in the academy's extensive horsemanship programs. Organized in 1897, the troop has taken part in eight presidential inaugurations, escorted kings and queens, and been featured in

Old Lighthouse Museum

major horse shows throughout the country, but you can see it free, with all its pomp and pageantry, each Sunday afternoon from May through October. That's when the troopers don their military dress, mount their black steeds and parade across the Academy's well-kept grounds. While you're there, pick up a map at the administration office and tour the 1,500-acre campus, beautifully situated near the shoreline of Lake Maxinkuckee. Contact Culver Military Academy, CEF 129, Culver 46511; (219) 842-3311.

Montgomery County

For sheer natural beauty, it's hard to beat **Shades State Park** near Waveland, but to fully appreciate its magnificent scenery and outstanding geologic features, you'll have to do some hiking. Only by taking to the trails can you see the primeval terrain for which the park is noted. Some first-time hikers do a double take when they see what awaits them—a landscape such as this just isn't associated with Indiana.

Some 470 acres of the 3,000-acre park have been set aside as the Pine Hills State Nature Preserve. Within its boundaries are four narrow rock ridges from 75 to 100 feet tall that are recognized as the finest example of incised meanders in the eastern United States. This observation was made by no less an authority than the National Park Service, which designated the preserve a National Natural Landmark.

Native white pine and hemlock, not usually found this far south, are relics of a long-ago past when this area was much cooler. The arrival of spring is first announced by the flowering of the rare snow trillium, and the coloring of the land continues through May, when the dogwoods and redbuds show off their blossoms. Through it all flows Sugar Creek, the most beautiful stream in the state.

When our forefathers first cast eyes on the lush forests and deep gorges along Sugar Creek, they referred to this place as "the Shades of Death." The deep shadows cast by the heavy growth of trees initially appeared ominous to them, but as they became more familiar with the area, the nickname was shortened to "the Shades." It remains appropriate to this day, since the land has remained virtually untouched by human hands.

Two other impressive features are the Silver Cascades Falls, one of eleven waterfalls in the park, and the Devil's Punchbowl, a large, circular grotto cut into the sandstone by two small streams.

Canoeists take to Sugar Creek in droves, and if you're into solitude, you'll want to avoid a trip on summer weekends. Weekdays in May or June or any day in August or September when the water level is down promise quieter floats. The most scenic stretch, which lies between Shades State Park and Turkey Run State Park (located to the southwest in adjoining Parke County), can be seen in one day. Put in at Deer's Mill Covered Bridge, which spans Sugar Creek along State Road 234 on the eastern edge of Shades State Park. For an enjoyable two-day trip, put in at Elston Park in Crawfordsville. Both trips end at West Union Covered Bridge in Parke County. Always check water conditions at park headquarters before starting out, however; the creek can be dangerous at flood stage.

Although most of the park is undeveloped, visitors will find more than one hundred primitive campsites, special campgrounds for backpackers and canoeists, and several picnic areas, some with shelters. Bicycles may be rented in the park, and a naturalist is on duty in the summer.

Shades State Park is located along both banks of Sugar Creek in southwestern Montgomery County and spills over into Parke County. The entrance is on County Road 800S, just west of State Road 234; look for signs. Open daily, year-round; nominal vehicle admission fee. Contact the Property Manager, Shades State Park, Route 1, Box 72, Waveland 47989; (317) 435–2810.

Just north of Shades State Park, County Road 875W leads north off State Road 234 to the Hoosier State's own Alamo, which the town's fifty residents hope you'll remember. There, on the outside front of an old school gymnasium, a local artist has created a series of colorful murals that depict both Alamos—the one in Texas and the one in Indiana.

Another small town in the northwestern corner of the county has recently achieved fame without even trying. When Hollywood came to Hoosierland looking for an idyllic rural area in which to film the principal exterior shots for the movie *Hoosiers,* it chose New Richmond. (For readers who missed it, *Hoosiers* is loosely based on the true story of a small town high school basketball team that defied all odds to win the Indiana state championship.) Now tourists, enthralled with what they saw on the screen, travel there to see the real thing—the storefronts, the main street with its single traffic light, the farm fields bathed in sunset gold. The sign that identifies the community as New Richmond is now embellished with the words, "Welcome to Hickory" (the town's movie name), and the Hickory Festival, held in late September, features a basketball game and *Hoosiers* film clips.

For information about Alamo and New Richmond, contact the Montgomery County Visitors & Convention Bureau, 211 South Washington Street, Crawfordsville 47933; (317) 362–6800.

The Old Montgomery County Jail at 225 North Washington Street in Crawfordsville was the first of only six rotary jails ever built and is the only one still operational. Completed in 1882, it remained in daily use until 1973. The cell blocks are arranged in a circle in such a way that the sheriff, with the turn of a crank, could rotate the cells around him and check on his prisoners without ever taking a step. Now known as the **Old Jail Museum,** it's open free of charge from 2:00 to 4:30 P.M., Thursday through Sunday, April through December, or by appointment; (317) 362–5222 or 362–6800.

The campus of Wabash College at the corner of West Wabash and Grant avenues in Crawfordsville is of interest because of the mid-1800s architecture of its buildings and its arboretum of native Indiana trees; (317) 362–1400.

Also in Crawfordsville, on the corner of Wallace Avenue and East Pike Street, you'll find a four-acre park that contains the study of General Lew Wallace. Famed as a lawyer, statesman, and Civil War general, Wallace is nevertheless probably best remembered as the author of the novel *Ben Hur.* His eclectic study, designed by Wallace himself, is a mix of French, Byzantine, Romanesque, and Greek styles. Each year in mid-October, a Circus Maximus is staged on these grounds, complete with a chariot race and Greek food. Open 1:00 to 5:00 P.M., Tuesday through Sunday, mid-April through October; nominal admission fee; (317) 362–5769.

Newton County

It's not true that nudists wear nothing at all—they wear shoes, watches, and insect repellent. You can see for yourself at the **Ponderosa Sun Club** north of Roselawn. Here sports buffs in the nude can play tennis and miniature golf. At the annual "Nudes A Poppin" show in July, judges select a Miss Nude Galaxy and the Nude Show Stopper of the Year; visitors, who are not required to disrobe, also see such special events as a nude mud-wrestling match between one guy and a three-gal tag team. Nude parties are held on most holidays, including New Year's Eve, and obviously, you don't have to worry about what to wear. Signs point the way from Roselawn to the club. For exact directions, visiting hours, and other information, contact the club at P.O. Box 305, Roselawn 46372; (219) 345–2268.

Porter County

Indiana does not have a Grand Canyon or a Yosemite, but it does have some of the largest sand dunes this side of the Sahara. Since 1972, most of them have been part of the 13,000-acre **Indiana Dunes National Lakeshore,** a miracle of survival in the midst of one of the most heavily industrialized regions of the country. Its lovely sand beaches along the southern shoreline of Lake Michigan are legendary for miles around, but they are only part of what can be seen and done here.

Mt. Baldy inches away from the lake each year; its name hints at the reason why. Because it has not been stabilized by vegetation, the 135-foot-tall dune is kept in constant motion by wind and water, forcing the dune to take giant step backward. Climb to the top for a sweeping view of Lake Michigan.

The landscape is not all sand and water. There are also grassy hills, patches of prairie, lush wetlands, and cool forests with a canopy so dense that sunlight barely filters through. Miller Woods, Cowles Bog, and Pinhook Bog would be exceptional natural areas anywhere, but their existence in the midst of such pollution, industry, and urban population is incredible.

The Bailly Homestead, dating to 1822, and the Chellberg Farm, built in the late 1880s, contain historical structures that the public may visit. There are hiking, bicycling, and horseback riding trails to follow; in the winter, they're used by cross-country skiers. At least 223 species of birds have been identified here, and many rare plants live among the dunes. Special programs and events are held all year long.

Although the national lakeshore actually lies in parts of three counties—Lake, Porter, and LaPorte—its visitor center is in Porter County, and this is where you should begin your visit. It is located on Kemil Road, which runs south from Highway 12 about 3 miles east of the intersection of Highway 12 and State Road 49 near Porter, and is open daily, year-round, 8:00 A.M. to 6:00 P.M. Memorial Day through Labor Day, 8:00 A.M. to 5:00 P.M. the rest of the year; closed major winter holidays. The park is open daily, year-round; hours vary from area to area and are subject to change. A nominal parking fee is charged at West Beach from Memorial Day through Labor Day; everything else is free. For additional information, contact Indiana Dunes National Lakeshore, 1100 North Mineral Springs Road, Porter 46304; (219) 926-7561.

Completely surrounded by the national lakeshore are 2,182 acres that make up **Indiana Dunes State Park.** It offers a microcosm of the features found in its big brother and boasts the highest sand dune along the lakeshore—192-foot-tall Mt. Tom. The 1,500-acre Dunes State Nature Preserve, which lies within park boundaries, contains more species of trees than any other area of comparable size in the Midwest; from one spot alone, you can identify thirty different varieties. In the summer, the myriads of rare flowers and ferns found here create a near-tropical appearance. Recreational facilities include a modern campground, nature center, a swimming beach, and trails for hiking, bicycling, and cross-country skiing. To reach the park, proceed north from Interstate 94 on State Road 49 for about 2 miles. The park is open year-round, but a nominal vehicle admission fee is charged only from spring through fall. Contact the Indiana Dunes State Park, 1600 North 25 East, Chesterton 46304; (219) 926-1952.

When the Chicago World's Fair of 1933 closed, five homes from the "Houses of the Future" exhibit were placed on a barge and transported across Lake Michigan to the then-new community of Beverly Shores. Plans to make Beverly Shores the ultimate vacation resort were thwarted by the Great Depression, but the houses are still there, lined up along Lake Front Drive, and still of interest. Especially startling is the **House of Tomorrow,** a twelve-sided structure built like a wedding cake (the top two floors are each smaller in circumference than the floor below). You'll also see a replica of Boston's Old North Church; it too was carted over from the Fair. For more information, contact the Porter County Convention, Recreation and Visitor Commission, 586 Indiana Oak Mall, Chesterton 46304; (219) 926-2255.

The magical kingdom of Oz is also a part of Dune Country. L. Frank Baum, author of the Oz books, used to summer here, and later, his son established the International Wizard of Oz Club in this area. Today, you can view a collection of Oz memorabilia in a free museum housed in the Yellow Brick Road shop in Chesterton. Open 10:00 A.M. to 5:00 P.M. Monday through Saturday. It's easy to find. Just follow the yellow brick road (honestly!) to 762 South Calumet Avenue; (219) 926–7048. Each September, a Wizard of Oz Festival, complete with several real-life Munchkins from the movie's original cast, evokes memories of the Judy Garland screen classic. Contact the Yellow Brick Road or the Chamber of Commerce, 107 Main Street, Chesterton 46304; (219) 926–5513.

The showpiece of Valparaiso in central Porter County is the striking Chapel of the Resurrection on the campus of Valparaiso University. This magnificent contemporary structure has received accolades from around the world. The entire building focuses on the chancel, whose limestone piers rise skyward for 98 feet and culminate in a roof shaped like a nine-point star. Try to visit here on a sunny day; from inside the chancel, the view of the awe-inspiring stained-glass windows will take your breath away. The largest Lutheran university in the country, Valparaiso counts the late Lowell Thomas among its alumni. Visitors are welcome at any time; the campus lies at the east end of Union Street; (219) 464–5093.

At Valparaiso Technical Institute, the **Wilbur H. Cummings Museum of Electronics** displays such artifacts as RCA's *Radiola* series of radios, televisions from the 40s, a 78-rpm Seeburg jukebox, and an Edison wax-cylinder player. It's located in Hershman Hall at 1 Center Street and is open free of charge from 9:00 A.M. to 4:00 P.M. Monday through Friday, 9:00 A.M. to noon Saturday; (219) 462–2191.

Housed in a facility that simulates a medieval village, Marc T. Nielsen Interiors, Inc. features craft shops for upholstery work, cabinet making, and furniture building in a Tudor-style farm structure. There's also a display of Old World furniture and accessories that may be unlike any you've ever seen. Virginia Phillips travels the world to buy the stunning collection of antiques. Store open 9:00 A.M. to 4:30 P.M. Monday through Friday; craft shops by appointment. Located at 734 North Old Suman Road near Valparaiso; (219) 462–9812.

At the Strongbow Turkey Inn, it's Thanksgiving all year long. You can have most any part of the gobbler cooked most any way imaginable here. Turkey appears in salads, soups, sandwiches, crepes, pies, and pâtés, not to mention sliced up on a plate and accompanied by all the traditional fixings. Everthing is made on the premises—breads, rolls, cranberry-orange relish, cakes, des-

sert pies, and a delicious cup custard. If you're in the mood for
something continental, try the veal Oscar, Coquilles St. Jacques,
or shrimp Pescatore. You'll find the inn at 2405 Highway 30 East,
Valparaiso. Open 11:00 A.M. to 9:00 P.M. Monday through Thursday, 11:00 A.M. to 10:00 P.M. Friday and Saturday, 11:00 A.M. to 8:00
P.M. Sunday; closed Christmas week. Reservations advised.

St. Joseph County

If you've ever wondered where all that spearmint in your Wrigley chewing gum comes from, here's your chance to find out. Call
the **Martin Blad Mint Farm** near South Bend and make an
appointment to visit them in July. That's when the bright yellow
mint wagons haul a newly harvested crop into the mint press
building. You can watch as the oil is separated, picked up, and
guided through coils, and pumped into fifty-five-gallon containers. Then it's packed up and sent off to Wrigley's en masse. The
2,500-acre farm is located at State Road 123, 1/2 mile north of its
junction with State Road 23, just southwest of South Bend. (219)
234–7271.

From nearly every vantage point in South Bend, you can see
the golden dome that tops the administration building of the University of Notre Dame. A walking tour of the 1,250-acre campus
will take you to such places as the Grotto of Our Lady of Lourdes,
an exact replica of the original in France; the Sacred Heart
Church, an awe-inspiring Gothic structure that contains one of
North America's oldest carillons; the Snite Museum of Art, which
houses rare religious artworks and masterpieces by European
and American artists; and the Notre Dame Memorial Library, a
huge, fourteen-story building noted for its rare book room and
the 132-foot-high mural that adorns its outer wall. To reach the
university, go north from South Bend on Highway 31/33 to
Angela Boulevard and turn east; call (219) 239–7367 for tour
information.

Of all the citizens of South Bend, past or present, Knute
Rockne is perhaps the best known. The famous coach, who
maintained that football was a game of brains rather than brawn,
shaped the Fighting Irish into a legend. When he died in a plane
crash in 1931, he was just forty-two years old. His funeral service,
attended by an estimated 100,000 people and carried by radio
across the nation and to Norway (the land of his birth), was one

of the most emotional in American history. You can visit his grave in Highland Cemetery, not far from his beloved university.

Also in the cemetery, located at 2557 Portage Avenue, is the giant Council Oak Tree. Estimated to be more than 400 years old, it's supported by a steel brace. La Salle and the Miami Indians signed a peace treaty beneath its sprawling branches in 1681.

Another name that's famous around South Bend is Studebaker. Clement Studebaker began his career as a wagon maker, making wagons for the Union Army during the Civil War and later for the thousands who trekked west. As he progressed from wagons to carriages to automobiles, he kept a collection of company vehicles. A portion of them are housed today in the Discovery Hall Museum at Century Center, 120 South St. Joseph Street, South Bend, among other memorabilia that depict the city's industrial history.

More Studebakers are on display in another South Bend museum at 520 South Lafayette Boulevard. Called the Studebaker Archives Center, it includes the Studebaker carriage in which Lincoln rode to the Ford Theatre the night he was assassinated.

Together, the two exhibits are known as the Studebaker National Museum. Both open from 10:00 A.M. to 4:30 P.M. Tuesday through Friday, 10:00 A.M. to 4:00 P.M. Saturday, 1:00 to 4:00 P.M. Sunday; closed Mondays and holidays. Nominal fee covers admission to both exhibits; half-price on Tuesday; (219) 284–9714.

By 1888, Studebaker had become a wealthy man, and he built himself a forty-room mansion worthy of his station, complete with twenty fireplaces and 24,000 square feet of space. Its massive stone walls, turrets, and irregular roofs gave it the appearance of a feudal castle. Today, the historic mansion is called Tippecanoe Place and houses a fine gourmet restaurant that serves continental cuisine. Lunch is available from 11:30 A.M. to 2:00 P.M. Monday through Friday; dinner from 5:00 to 10:00 P.M. Monday through Thursday, 5:00 to 11:00 P.M. Friday, 4:30 to 11:00 P.M. Saturday, 4:00 to 9:00 P.M. Sunday. A Sunday brunch is served buffet-style from 9:00 A.M. to 2:00 P.M. Located at 620 West Washington Street; (219) 234–9077. Tours are available outside of dining hours.

The only artificial white-water course in North America and one of only three in the world is located in the heart of downtown South Bend. Called the East Race Waterway, it's a 2,000-foot-long channel that bypasses the South Bend Dam across the St. Joseph River. The elite of white-water paddlers from around the globe come here each summer to take part in national and international competitions. Because the flow of water can be controlled, the waterway can generate the churning rapids and 6-foot-tall waves needed for athletic events or present a surface calm enough for whole families to embark upon. It's open to the public for inner-tubing, rafting, and other water sports, under the watchful eyes of a well-trained rescue team, for approximately thirty hours per week throughout the summer; hours vary. The many adjacent walkways and bridges provide landlubbers with a close-up view of waterway happenings. Located east of the St. Joseph River, along the west side of Niles Avenue and between Jefferson Boulevard on the south and Madison Street on the north. For additional information, contact the East Race Waterway Sports and Recreation Corp., 401 East Colfax Avenue, South Bend 46617; (219) 233–6121.

The East Race Waterway also functions as a fish ladder (the first of four ladders planned for the St. Joseph River) during spawning season. Eventually, steelhead trout and Chinook salmon will be able to detour around four dams and travel freely along the 63-mile stretch of river between Mishawaka and Lake Michigan. Some 600,000 of those fish will be reared annually at the Twin Branch State Fish Hatchery in Mishawaka. Visitors may take a free, self-guided tour of the facilities between 8:00 A.M. and 4:00 P.M. any day of the year. Located at 13200 East Jefferson Boulevard; (219) 255–4199.

In Mishawaka, the **100 Center Complex** of shops, restaurants, art galleries, and theatres occupies the original buildings of the Kamm & Schellinger Brewery (c. 1853). Located on the south bank of the St. Joseph River at 700 Lincolnway West; (219) 259–7861. The *Princess,* a sternwheeler paddleboat that docks at the Center, offers daily cruises between Mishawaka and South Bend from May through mid-October; (219) 259–6080.

Tippecanoe County

On November 7, 1811, William Henry Harrison, then Governor of the Indiana Territory, led his men in battle against the last all-Indian army to be assembled east of the Mississippi River. The Indians, representing a confederacy of tribes organized by Tecumseh and his brother, the Prophet, went down in defeat, ending any organized Indian resistance to the white man's settlement of the Northwest Territory. In later years, Harrison's victory was a prominent factor in his successful bid for the presidency of the United States.

You can see an impressive 85-foot-tall monument and stroll the 96-acre grounds where the battle was actually fought at the Tippecanoe Battlefield State Memorial near the town of Battle Ground. A scenic trail leads past several trees that stood during the battle; musket balls are still found in the older trees when they fall. The park is also a peaceful and lovely spot for a picnic—except on those summer weekends when two noisy annual events take place. Dulcimers, guitars, mandolins, and more hold all-day, all-night jam sessions during the Indiana Fiddlers' Gathering; less lyrical sounds fill the air when various types of old machinery rev up their motors at the Antique Farm Power Show. The park is open daily, free of charge, year-round during daylight hours. A museum on the grounds presents the history of the battle from both sides' point of view; open 10:00 A.M. to 5:00 P.M. Monday through Saturday, 1:00 to 5:00 P.M. Sunday, closed in January; nominal admission fee. Located on Prophet's Rock Road just west of Battle Ground; follow signs; (317) 567–2147.

On certain nights, full moon or not, you can join a howling at Battle Ground's **Wolf Park.** The eerie but beautiful voices of the resident wolf pack drift through the air and send chills up and down your spine. If you like these misunderstood creatures, it is an experience you will never forget.

This unique wildlife park is a research facility, and you may visit during the day to watch scientists at work. Docents are on hand to tell you each wolf's name and rank order in the pack, and you can see the wolves interact with humans whom the wolves have accepted as members of their "society." Each Saturday and Sunday at 2:00 P.M., predators (wolves) and prey (bison) are placed together to demonstrate that a healthy animal has nothing to fear from wolves.

The park is operated by the nonprofit North American Wildlife Park Foundation, which charges a nominal admission fee to the park to help offset expenses. Advance reservations are required for the howls. The park is open 1:00 to 5:00 P.M. Saturday and Sunday from the first weekend in May to November 30; howls are held year-round. To reach the park, go north from Battle Ground on Harrison Road for about 1 mile; Wolf Park signs point the way. Write Wolf Park, c/o North American Wildlife Park Foundation, Battle Ground 47920; (317) 567–2265.

In Lafayette, the twenty-acre **Clegg Memorial Garden** perches on the high bank of Wildcat Creek. Wander along a mile of marked trails that lead past ancient white oaks, sugar maples, and dogwoods. Daffodils bloom in the spring; hybrid day lilies unfold their petals in June and July, followed by resurrection lilies in August and Japanese anemones in September. From Lookout Point, you can see the Indiana countryside for miles around. Open 10:00 A.M. to sunset daily; free. Located at 1854 North County Road 400 East; (317) 742–0325.

Off the Beaten Path in Southeast Indiana

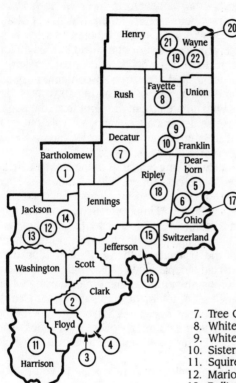

1. North Christian Church/ Otter Creek Clubhouse
2. Huber Orchard, Winery, and U-Pick Farm
3. Riverside City Park/Wave-Tek Water Park
4. Howard Steamboat Museum
5. Hillforest Mansion
6. Red Wolf Sanctuary
7. Tree City Fall Festival
8. Whitewater Valley Railroad
9. Whitewater Canal
10. Sisters of St. Francis
11. Squire Boone Caverns
12. Marion-Kay Products
13. Bell's Ford Bridge
14. Muscatatuck National Wildlife Refuge
15. United Nations of the Poultry World
16. Lanier mansion
17. *Hoosier Boy*
18. Tyson Methodist Church
19. Webb's Antique Mall
20. Levi Coffin House
21. Tedco, Inc.
22. Hayes Regional Arboretum

Southeast Indiana

Bartholomew County

According to an article that appeared in the *New York Times Magazine* in recent years, "there is really no equivalent of Columbus anywhere." That's just one of many tributes this town of 35,000 people has received from around the world in recognition of its architecture. More than forty public and private buildings make up the most concentrated collection of contemporary architecture on earth, and the names of the architects, artists, designers, and sculptors who created them are right from the pages of *Who's Who*. Where else, for instance, can you walk out of a church designed by Eliel Saarinen, cross the street, pass a Henry Moore sculpture, and enter a library designed by I. M. Pei?

One of the most visually striking buildings is the **North Christian Church,** designed by Eero Saarinen. A low, hexagon-shaped building, it has a sloping roof centered by a towering, needlelike spire. The multilevels of Smith Elementary School, created by John M. Johansen, are connected by several brightly colored, tube-shaped ramps—pure delight for the children who use them. The new sanctuary of the St. Paul's Lutheran Church, topped by an 85-foot-tall, copper-clad steeple, rises in Byzantine-like splendor above its surroundings—beautiful at any time, dazzling when touched by the sun. Just east of town, the sprawling **Otter Creek Clubhouse** designed by Harry Weese lies adjacent to one of the finest public golf courses in the country; Robert Trent Jones, who laid out the course, says its thirteenth hole is the single best hole he's ever designed.

Not all of these buildings will knock the socks off you at first sight. To fully appreciate them, you should learn something about the innovative functions and attention to details that lie behind the facades. Many amaze you when you learn the years in which they were constructed; the First Christian Church, built in 1942, could just as easily have been built yesterday.

Columbus also has its share of renovations and historical buildings, but it is the modern architecture that has brought this small town fame as the "Athens of the Prairie."

Begin your tour at the Columbus Visitors Center, housed in a nineteenth-century home at 506 Fifth Street, where you can pick

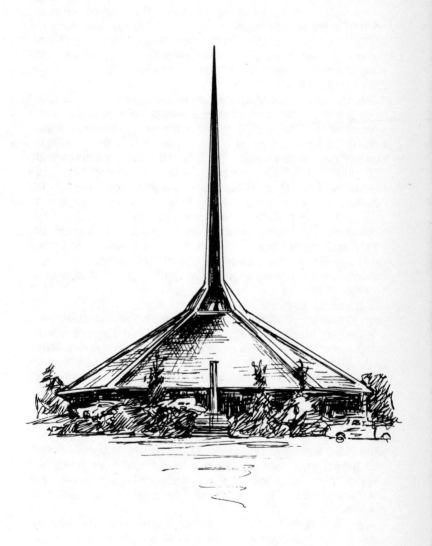

North Christian Church

up maps and descriptive cassette tapes for self-guided tours. Reservations may also be made in advance for a minibus guided tour, available daily April through October. The Visitors Center is open 9:00 A.M. to 5:00 P.M. Monday through Saturday and noon to 4:00 P.M. Sunday, April through October; closed Sunday the rest of the year. For additional information, write Columbus Area Visitor Information, 825 Washington Street, Columbus 47201; (812) 378–2622 or 372–1954.

There's nothing contemporary about Zaharako's Confectionery in downtown Columbus—it's pure nostalgia. Located at the same address since October 1900, the store is now a Columbus institution. Its fixtures carry you back to the first of the century—Mexican onyx soda fountains purchased from the St. Louis World Exposition in 1905, a full concert mechanical pipe organ brought here from Germany in 1908, which rings out with tunes of the Gay Nineties, an exquisite Tiffany lamp, accessories of carved mahogany. Amid these ornate surroundings, you can enjoy homemade ice cream, fountain treats, and an assortment of candy and sandwiches. You'll find it at 329 Washington Street, (812) 379–9329, right across the street from Columbus's ultramodern, award-winning shopping mall, the Commons, designed by Cesar Pelli.

Completely enclosed, the Commons houses a unique playground that your children will want to take home with them and a seven-ton, in-motion sculpture crafted by Jean Tinguely out of scrap metal that becomes more intriguing the longer you look at it.

Not far southwest of Columbus, there's a KOA campground where you might want to spend not just a night, but a whole vacation. Certainly all the makings are there—lovely shaded campsites, a swimming pool, free movies, projection TV, a fishing lake, a small grocery store, and a nature trail. Every Saturday night from Memorial Day weekend through Halloween country and gospel music set your toes a-tappin' and your hands a-clappin'. Many other special events are scheduled, too, such as free ham and bean dinners, hayrides, ice cream socials, and flea markets.

Larry and Betty York, who own the campground, also have a sideline that has developed into a local spectator event. Every night at approximately 8:00 P.M., from mid-June to the first frost, everyone gathers around the Yorks' flower box to await the blooming of the spinning Persian primroses. A few minutes later, the yellow flowers begin their nightly transformation; it takes exactly five seconds for each one to develop from pods to 4-inch blooms. The blossoms last until about noon the following day, and by evening, there are new flowers to open.

The family of the campground's former owner, John Marr, began raising the primroses when John's grandmother brought one home from a trip (no one can remember where), but didn't realize until some time later that they had what was probably the only plant of its type in Indiana. And to judge by the reactions of campers from all across the country, they're not all that well known anywhere else, either. Out of more than 60,000 visitors, two have said they've seen these flowers elsewhere. Those statistics are changing, however. The Yorks sell the plants for $3 each in their campground store, and campers who return home with them report good luck in both growing primroses and astonishing neighbors. You don't have to be a camper to own a primrose, though—the store is open to noncampers as well. Both store and campground are open year-round. Write the Columbus KOA, 8855 South 300W, Columbus 47201; (812) 342-6229.

Clark County

Along the bank of the Ohio River in Clarksville lies a 375-million-year-old fossil bed that is one of the world's great natural wonders. Its rare and unusual formations date back to the Devonian age and have for decades attracted sightseers and scientists from around the world. Once the reef was covered by the Falls of the Ohio, a raging, 2-mile stretch of water below Louisville in which the Ohio River dropped 22 feet over limestone ledges. Now the Ohio has been reduced to a series of pools by a string of dams, and the controlled water levels have left the reef high and dry. Its fossil corals archaeological sites are among the best in the country, and the variety of its migratory bird life is unparalleled at any other inland location.

For years, efforts have been underway to preserve this area. The first step in realizing that dream occurred in October 1984, when the U.S. Senate approved funding for the creation of the Falls of the Ohio National Wildlife Preservation Area. In the spring of 1988, it was announced that the U.S. Army Corps of Engineers will acquire 1,404 acres of land for the area, and the state of Indiana will manage the property as a state park. Until plans can be formulated, access to the fossil bed—believed to be the largest exposed coral reef in the world—is available at Clarksville's **Riverside City Park,** open free of charge from dawn to dusk. The park lies on the south side of Riverside Drive, about 1 mile west of Highway 31-E. For a panoramic view of the reef and the Ohio River, visit the George Rogers Clark State Historic Site at 1024 West Harrison Avenue in Clarksville. It's open daily, free of charge, during daylight hours. Additional information can be provided by the Clark-Floyd Counties Convention and Tourism Bureau, 540 Marriott Drive (P.O. Box 608), Clarksville 47131; (812) 282–6654.

When you don't have any ocean waves close at hand, there's only one thing to do—create your own. And that's just what they've done at **Wave-Tek Water Park** in Clarksville. In addition to the Olympic-size pool where 3-foot waves ripple the surface every few minutes, there's also the Water Boggan, a giant water slide that hurtles you down a toboggan-style flume, and the Rampage, a giant water roller coaster. Although it's part of the Marriott Inn Complex, the water park is open to the general public. Marriott Inn is located at 505 Marriott Drive; take the Stanisfer Avenue exit off Interstate 65. The water park is open 11:00 A.M. to 6:00 P.M. daily, as well as 6:30 to 9:00 P.M. on Monday, Thursday, and Saturday, mid-May through Labor Day. Various admission fees depend on the facilites you use and how long you use them; (812) 283–4411.

Presiding over Clarksville is the town's own version of London's Big Ben. The main building of the Colgate-Palmolive plant at State and Woerner streets is topped by the second largest clock in the world, a monstrous 40 feet in diameter with a 16-foot-long hour hand that weighs 500 pounds. (The largest clock, 50 feet in diameter, sits atop Colgate's plant in Jersey City, NJ) No one in Clarksville gets away with saying he doesn't know the time—the electric-powered clock is reputed to be accurate to within 15 seconds a month, and the clock's face can be read from a distance of $2^{1/2}$ miles.

You may take a free tour of Colgate's facilities at 9:00 A.M. each Tuesday if you make an advance appointment; call Employee Relations at (812) 283–6611. The plant, which produces an array of household and personal care products, is housed in a building that served as Indiana's first state prison.

Jeffersonville, which adjoins Clarksville to the east, is home to the biggest inland boatbuilders in the country. You can see them at work, usually building barges, along the waterfront.

Until 1931, the Howard Shipyards were here. During their 107 years in business, the yards produced some 3,000 steamboats, reported to be the finest ever to ply the waters of North America and Central America. The *J. M. White,* the most luxurious steamboat in history, was built here, as were the *Glendy Burke,* which inspired the Stephen Foster song of the same name; the *City of Louisville,* the fastest steamboat ever built; and the *Cape Girardeau,* captured on film for all time in *Gone With the Wind.*

The steamboat era was flourishing in the 1890s when construction began on the elaborate twenty-two-room Howard mansion at 1101 East Market Street that today houses the **Howard Steamboat Museum.** A striking late-Victorian structure, the house features stained- and leaded-glass windows, a Moorish-style music room that contains its original nee-Louis XV furniture, and intricate embellishments that were hand carved from fifteen different types of wood.

You can see all this today, plus a priceless collection of relics that played a role in the golden era of steamboating, miniature models of Howard-built steamboats and whole rooms furnished like staterooms on the finest turn-of-the-century boats. Guided tours are available beginning at 10:00 A.M. Tuesday through Saturday and at 1:00 P.M. Sunday; last tour starts at 3:00 P.M. Nominal admission fee; write the Clark County Historical Society at P.O. Box 606, Jeffersonville 47130, or call (812) 283–3728 for further details.

If all this reminiscing puts you in the mood to actually take to the river, arrange a cruise aboard the *Bonnie Belle.* The authentic sternwheeler is pure river lore come to life. Docked at the foot of Spring Street in Jeffersonville, she departs for sightseeing tours at 1:30 P.M. daily and for dinner cruises at 7:00 P.M. Wednesday through Sunday from May through October. Schedule may vary; call (812) 282–9500 for reservations and latest information.

Breathes there a man alive who never to himself has said (at least in the days of his youth), "Boy, would I love to have a Louisville Slugger!" One would think, of course, that they're made in Louisville, but such is not the case. The world-famous hardwood bats, some 5 million of them each year, are manufactured at the Hillerich and Bradsby Company plant in Jeffersonville.

Most are shaped on semiautomatic lathes, but those used by professional baseball players are still handturned by the most skilled of craftsmen. According to a company executive, the custom-made models are necessary because a pro can tell the difference of a fraction of an ounce in weight or of a sixteenth of an inch in the handle size. During the free tour, you'll even receive a miniature 18-inch-long Louisville Slugger to commemorate your visit.

Die-hard baseball fans will especially enjoy the company's Bat Museum, which contains Sluggers used by the most famous players in history. One was used by Ty Cobb during his last week in the majors. Yet another was used by Babe Ruth to hit twenty-one home runs, and he personally notched his bat for each one. You'll also see bats once swung by such notables as Pete Rose, Hank Aaron, and Lou Gehrig.

The museum is open 8:00 A.M. to noon and 1:00 to 3:30 P.M. Monday through Friday; plant tours are conducted twice daily, Monday through Friday; the plant is closed the last three days in June, the first two weeks in July and Christmas week. Call the tour director at (812) 288–6611 for exact tour times (they vary with the season). The plant, known as Slugger Park, also produces Power Bilt golf clubs. Located at 1525 Charlestown-New Albany Rd., just off Interstate 65 at the Cementville/Clarksville exit.

Something's always going on at the 450-acre Huber Farm near Borden. Officially billed as the **Huber Orchard, Winery, and U-Pick Farm,** it's open to the public year-round. Strawberries are ripe for the picking from mid-May through mid-June. Twelve varieties of apples are in season from late summer through December. You can select your own pumpkin right from the patch in the fall and cut your own Christmas tree in December. Cider made on the farm each fall is available for purchase at any time.

Brothers Gerald and Carl Huber, along with their families, have turned their talents to commercial winemaking in recent years, and thus far, they've garnered more than fifty awards for their efforts, including "Best of Show" at the 1983 Indiana State Fair. Visitors are welcome to sample their seventeen varieties and tour the winery. You can buy the makings of a picnic lunch, as well as ready-made sandwiches and cheese trays, right on the farm. The winery and gift shop are open daily year-round, but hours vary. Call (812) 923–9813 or 923–9463 for hours and exact directions, or write the Hubers at RR 1, Box 202, Borden 47106.

Just down the road, on a 360-acre farm, is the Joe Huber Family Restaurant. The down-home country cooking, which features fried chicken, fried biscuits, and fresh fruit and vegetables, is served family style. Open 11:00 A.M. to 9:00 P.M. Monday through Saturday; 11:00 A.M. to 6:00 P.M. Sunday, March through December; (812) 923–5255.

Dearborn County

Atop a wooded hillside overlooking the village of Aurora stands a splendid yellow frame house filled with the memories of a bygone era. It was built in the 1850s by Thomas Gaff, a wealthy industrialist and shipping magnate whose steamboats regularly plied the waters of the Ohio River far below.

Gaff's love for the river ran deep, and that love is reflected in his home, **Hillforest Mansion,** whose architectural style is often referred to as "steamboat Gothic." And indeed it does resemble a steamboat in part, with its rounded front porticos and cupola, coupled columns and suspended interior staircase—all features that were typical of the "floating palaces" that graced our country's rivers in the heyday of river transportation.

Now restored and filled with antique furniture, the entire mansion can be toured, from its wine cellar up to the observatory at the top of the house. The view of the Ohio River is just as beautiful as it was when Thomas Gaff himself stood here. Around the one-of-a-kind home are ten acres of grounds, laid out in the grand manner of an Italian villa. Open 1:00 to 5:00 P.M., Tuesday through Sunday, May through December 23; admission fee; situated at 213 Fifth Street; (812) 926-0087.

About 2¹/₂ miles west of Aurora on Highway 50, you'll find an attractive restaurant built around a living tree called, appropriately enough, The Tree House. Hanging plants, brick archways, and a glass roof contribute to the garden atmosphere. Specialties of the house include barbecued ribs, veal Parmesan, seafood, filet mignon, and prime rib, which, at dinnertime, will cost you from about $7–$14. Buffets are offered Friday night and Sunday. Children's menu available; reservations recommended. Open 11:00 A.M. to 9:00 P.M. Sunday and Tuesday through Thursday; 11:00 A.M. to 10:00 P.M. Friday and Saturday; closed Monday, January 1, and December 25; (812) 926-3737.

Named for an animal now extinct in the wild, the **Red Wolf Sanctuary** near Dillsboro is home to several red and gray wolves, coyotes, foxes, a mountain lion, and an assortment of raptors. The red wolves seen here are hybrids (part coyote)—the few remaining pure red wolves in this country live on lands managed by the U.S. Fish and Wildlife Service.

Established more than ten years ago by Paul Strasser, a former zookeeper, the twenty-three-acre refuge also serves as a rehabilitation center for sick and injured wildlife from all over the country. Paul and his wife Jane nurse their wild charges back to health, returning those who fully recuperate to their natural habitats and adding the others to their growing "family."

The Strassers welcome visitors to their sanctuary free of charge from Thursday through Sunday year-round, but they request that you call in advance and make an appointment. If you want to see the newborn young, come in the spring. Located approximately 5 miles southwest of Dillsboro via State Road 62. Contact the sanctuary at P.O. Box 235, Dillsboro 47018; (812) 667–5303.

Decatur County

It's easy to tell the visitors from the hometown folks in Greensburg—the visitors are all looking up. Up at a tree that's growing where we've all been led to believe trees can't grow—on a roof. Eyecatching, to be sure.

The tree adorns the tower that tops the Decatur County Courthouse. When the first tree appeared here in 1870, local authorites, who knew a tree's proper place, grubbed it out. Five years later, a second tree appeared. The amazed citizenry, admiring its tenacity, merely stood by and watched this time. That tree thrived until 1929, when it failed to leaf and was removed to the local Decatur County Museum for preservation.

At the time of its removal, another tree had already started growing on the opposite side of the tower. It was later joined by a second tree, so that today there are actually two trees, both growing without any apparent nourishment (although local comedians conjecture that they are fed by the springs in the tower's clock). The townsfolk have long since made their peace with this peculiar situation, and they even celebrate each September with a **Tree City Fall Festival.**

What type of tree had implanted itself on the courthouse roof? For years, no one could agree on the answer, and finally scientists at the Smithsonian Institution in Washington, D.C., were consulted. They declared the trees to be large tooth aspens. For additional information, write the Greensburg Area Chamber of Commerce, 125 West Main Street, Greensburg 47240; (812) 663–2832.

Fayette County

The **Whitewater Valley Railroad,** longest steam railroad in Indiana, travels 32 scenic miles between Connersville and Metamora (see Franklin County) each Saturday, Sunday, and holiday from May through November. All the sights and sounds of old-time steam travel have been re-created to transport you back in time, and places of interest are pointed out along the way. Two rare Baldwin locomotives, vintage 1907 and 1919, pull New York Central and Erie Stillwell passenger cars over tracks laid along the towpath of the old Whitewater Canal. At Metamora, there's time to disembark and explore a restored canal town.

Both round- and one-way trips, as well as caboose rides and special Christmas runs, are available. Round trips, which are approximately five hours long, originate at the Connersville station, located 1 mile south of town on State Road 121. Write the Whitewater Valley Railroad, Inc., P.O. Box 406, Connersville 47331; (317) 825–2054.

Seven miles southwest of Connersville on County Road 350S is the Mary Gray Bird Sanctuary, a 684–acre wildlife preserve owned and operated by the Indiana Audubon Society. These peaceful surroundings are crisscrossed by several miles of hiking trails, and a fulltime naturalist is on hand to answer your questions. A small museum depicts local flora and fauna. The preserve is open daily, free of charge, from dawn to dusk. Contact the sanctuary at RR 6, Box 165, Connersville 47331; (317) 825–9788.

Franklin County

Not too long ago, Metamora was a dying town, its days numbered by the end of the canal era. That was before the state of Indiana decided to restore a 14-mile section of the old **Whitewater Canal,** orginally a 76-mile waterway constructed in the mid-1800s, and now the small village hums with activity.

An 80-foot-long wooden aqueduct in Metamora was built in 1848 to carry the canal 16 feet above Duck Creek. Believed to be the only such structure in existence, it was once featured in Ripley's "Believe It or Not."

Whitewater Valley Railroad

A horse-drawn canal boat takes visitors for a leisurely 30-minute cruise through the aqueduct and a restored lock. Occasionally, the Whitewater Valley Railroad's steam train chugs by, carrying passengers between its Connersville station and Metamora (see Fayette County).

Many of the town's fine arts, crafts, and specialty shops are housed in pre-Civil War buildings that cling to the banks of the canal; others occupy reconstructed and reproduced buildings elsewhere in a section known as Old Metamora. An aged brick grist mill still grinds and sells flour, cornmeal, and grits. The total effect is that of a country village suspended in the 1830s.

Of the many special events scheduled throughout the year, the loveliest is the Christmas Walk that's held evenings on the first three Fridays and Saturdays after Thanksgiving. Some 3,000 luminaries line the banks of the canal, roads, and walkways. Carolers stroll through the streets; horses clippity clop along, pulling carriages behind them. The aroma of hot, spiced cider perfumes the air. Quite a show for a town that has a population of about sixty permanent residents!

Most shops are open 10:00 A.M. to 5:00 P.M. Tuesday through Friday and 9:00 A.M. to 6:00 P.M. Saturday, Sunday, and holidays, from mid-April to mid-December, while some are open on weekends only. For additional information, contact the Metamora Visitor Center, Box 117, Metamora 47030; (317) 647–2109.

The canal boat operates from noon to 3:30 P.M. Tuesday through Friday, 10:30 A.M. to 5:45 P.M. Saturday and 11:30 A.M. to 5:45 P.M. Sunday, June through October; a nominal fee is charged. Write the Whitewater Canal State Memorial, Box 88, Metamora 47030; (317) 647–6512.

Oldenburg is another architectural and historical gem that has dwelt in the last century since it was founded in 1837. Known as the "Village of Spires" because of its many soaring steeples, Oldenburg is the home of the convent and academy of the **Sisters of St. Francis,** an order that originally came here from Austria. The peaceful grounds, which invite leisurely strolls, include a cemetery reserved for the Sisters. In warm weather months, the cemetery is a stunning mosaic in green and white—paths edged by low-cut green hedges, emerald lawns shaded by the sprawling branches of ancient shade trees, and row upon row of small, white stone crosses that are identical to each other. The convent itself, renowned for its ceiling frescoes, basilica-like chapel, iron stairways, and solid oak woodwork, may be toured by appointment. Call (812) 934–2475.

Elsewhere in the picturesque community are houses and store-fronts adorned with the ornate tinwork of master craftsman Gasper Gaupel. The lovely, tree-lined streets bear German names, ranging from the mundane Haupstrasse (Main Street) to the lyrical Schweineschwantz Gasse (Pigtail Alley). Every so often, the aroma of brats and sauerkraut escapes from a local eatery. If you'd like to sample some German cuisine, just follow your nose.

Harrison County

A few miles south of Corydon, there's a peaceful valley laced with subterranean caverns and edged by forested hills. Squire Boone first saw this area in the late 1700s while hunting with his older brother, Daniel, and eventually returned here to settle down, building a home for his family and a grist mill that provided their means of support. When he died in 1815, he was buried at his own request in the cave that today bears his name, and the walnut coffin that contains his remains may be seen on a guided tour.

Squire Boone Caverns offer a wondrous mix of colorful stalactites and stalagmites, underground streams, waterfalls, twisted helictites, massive pillars of stone, and the world's largest travertine dam formation. Cave crickets, blind crayfish, isopods, amphipods, and a few bats live in the cave's deepest recesses. The tour guides are extremely well informed about this cave and caves in general. At one point along the way, in the belly of the cave, all lights are turned out—an eerie experience that gives new meaning to the word black. This is not the largest cave around, but it is certainly one of the most dazzling. Visitors should be aware that the subterranean temperature is a constant 54 degrees, and there is a steep spiral staircase to climb at the end of the fifty-five minute, 1/3-mile tour.

Topside, you can visit an operating grist mill rebuilt on the original foundation used by Squire Boone, watch the miller at work, and buy his products. A cluster of log cabins near the cave's entrance houses various craft shops, an art gallery, a homemade-candy store, and a restaurant; the craftsmen who work here are as authentic as the log cabins that shelter them. Children can get acquainted with farm animals at a petting zoo.

Although it's small in size and limited in menu, the restaurant serves some of the finest homemade soups, sandwiches, salads, and desserts in southern Indiana. Even the coffee and iced tea are exceptional, and the restaurant itself is bright, airy, clean, and cheerful.

To reach Squire Boone Caverns and Village, go south from Corydon on State Road 135 for about 10 miles, then turn east on Squire Boone Caverns Road for another 3 miles; look for signs. Cave tours are offered 9:00 A.M. to 6:00 P.M. daily, May through October; 9:30 A.M. to 5:00 P.M., March through April and November through December; 10:00 A.M. to 5:00 P.M. Saturday and Sunday the rest of the year; closed major winter holidays. Squire Boone Village is open 10:00 A.M. to 6:00 P.M. daily from Memorial Day weekend through Labor Day weekend and from 11:00 A.M. to 5:00 P.M. each Saturday and Sunday thereafter through October. Admission fee. The grist mill, which lies just outside the cave-village complex, is open, free of charge, when the village is open. Write P.O. Box 411, Corydon 47112; (812) 732–4381.

Back in Corydon at the Zimmerman Art Glass Co., you can observe a process that is now nearly extinct. Brothers Bart and Kerry Zimmerman hand blow every piece of glassware they make, and no two are identical. The Zimmermans specialize in paperweights—clear crystal balls, large and small, that enclose unfolding blossoms—but will try just about anything that tickles their fancy. Their glass menagerie includes trays of glass fruits, sugar bowls and creamers, an assortment of baskets, lamps, vases, and perfume decanters—some clear, some in exquisite color.

Many customers order items made to their specifications, like the lady from Australia who dropped by to describe the lamp she wanted and asked the partners to send it to her home—the shipping charges cost more than the lamp.

Although small, the company is nationally known, and its artistic wares are displayed in many museums, including the Smithsonian Institution. You're welcome to drop in and watch these skilled craftsmen breathe life into molten glass; free glass-sculpting demonstrations are given from 9:00 to 9:30 A.M. each business day. The factory, open from 8:00 A.M. to 4:00 P.M. Tuesday through Saturday except major holidays, is housed in a green, corrugated-metal shed at 395 Valley Road, right next to the Arpac poultry-processing plant on the south edge of Corydon; (812) 738–2206.

The Louisville, New Albany & Corydon Railroad is one of the shortest railroads in the nation—its entire track is just under 8 miles in length. Established in 1883, "The Dinky," as it's affectionately known to local residents, has been hauling freight from Corydon to Corydon Junction ever since. Railroad enthusiasts may accompany the engineer and crew on a 16-mile round trip by special arrangement. The depot at Walnut and Water streets in Corydon displays antique railroad equipment; (812) 738–3171.

Jackson County

The heavenly aroma that sometimes tantalizes the nostrils in Brownstown is a vanilla bean on its way to becoming vanilla extract. This metamorphosis takes place each working day at the **Marion-Kay Products** plant, which turns out an array of spices and seasonings. You can learn about the whole process, as well as the history of spices, on a free tour. The Marion-Kay plant lies along Highway 50 on the western edge of town. Open 8:00 A.M. to 4:30 P.M. Monday through Friday; call (812) 358–3000 for tour hours.

Indiana's Skyline Drive meanders across a series of knobs for some 6 miles through the Jackson-Washington State Forest and offers some spectacular hilltop vistas. The poorly surfaced road is very hilly and treacherous, so plan on taking your time. To reach the drive, head south from Brownstown on South Poplar Street and follow the signs. Write the Jackson-Washington State Forest, R.R. 2, Brownstown 47220, or call (812) 358–2160, for information about the drive and the many recreational opportunities elsewhere in the forest.

Jackson County has the finest collection of long covered bridges in the state. Three of them span the East Fork of the White River. To view what's billed as one of the longest covered bridges in the world, head east from Medora for 1 mile on State Road 235. The 434-foot-long span, built in 1875, is certainly the longest in Indiana. It carried traffic across the river until 1974, when it was bypassed by a new bridge. Sadly, the old Medora Bridge is slowly falling into decay—the cost to preserve it has thus far been out of reach.

The 325-foot-long **Bell's Ford Bridge** is the only triple burr arch-covered bridge in Indiana and the only known Post truss bridge in existence anywhere. Erected in 1869, the Post truss represents a period when bridges were evolving from all-wood into all-metal or concrete structures. Its sides and floor feature iron rods and straps covered with wood. Located on State Road 258 3 miles west of Seymour.

The Shieldstown Covered Bridge, constructed in 1876, is 331 feet long. To visit it, go southwest from Seymour on Highway 50 for about 6½ miles, then turn northwest onto a country road leading to Crane Hill and proceed about 1 mile; look for signs along the way.

For additional information about the county's bridges, contact the Seymour Chamber of Commerce, 105 South Chestnut Street (P.O. Box 312), Seymour 47274; (812) 522–3681.

Wildlife lovers will want to stop at **Muscatatuck National Wildlife Refuge,** located 3 miles east of Seymour on the south side of Highway 50. Covering more than 7,700 acres, it's Indiana's only such refuge and was established primarily as a sanctuary for wood ducks. Each spring and fall, thousands of migrating waterfowl pause to rest on the open water, joined occasionally by flocks of sandhill cranes. White-tailed deer and wild turkeys make their homes here all year long. The refuge is open daily, year-round, from dawn to dusk; nominal admission fee. Write Muscatatuck National Wildlife Refuge, Route 7, Box 189A, Seymour 47274; (812) 522–4352.

Jefferson County

Charles Kuralt once called Madison the most beautiful river town in America. The curator of a Michigan museum said, when he first saw Madison, "Put a fence around the entire town and don't let anyone touch anything in it!" During World War II, the Office of War Information selected Madison as the "typical American town" and made movies of it in thirty-two languages to distribute around the world and to remind our troops what they were fighting for. The old *Life* magazine chose Madison as the most pleasant small town in the country in which to live. Its nineteenth-century architecture, a mix of several styles, has been praised as the most beautiful in the Midwest, and its setting on the banks of the Ohio River, against a backdrop of wooded hills and limestone bluffs, is equally lovely. Obviously, if you're going to tour Indiana, Madison is one place you shouldn't miss.

Once Madison was a thriving river port and the largest town in the state. When railroads arrived on the scene, the river traffic departed, and Madison, in keeping with the times, built its own railroad. What no one foresaw was that nearly everyone would get on the train and leave town. For many years, no one came to replace the populace that had moved on to greener pastures, and 133 blocks of buildings thus survived an era when it was fashionable to tear down anything old and replace it with something new in the name of progress. It is this legacy of architectural splendor that may be seen today.

The most notable building is the **Lanier mansion** at 511 West First Street, a palatial mansion built in the 1840s for about $50,000—quite a chunk of money in those days. Its owner, James Lanier, was an astute banker whose loans to the state government during the Civil War helped Indiana avert bankruptcy. Facing a broad lawn that rambles down to the Ohio River, the Lanier mansion is an outstanding example of the Greek Revival style. Its two-story portico is supported by tall Corinthian columns and hemmed in by wrought-iron grillwork. Inside, a spiral staircase climbs three stories, unsupported except by its own thrust, and each of the rooms is decorated with period furniture and accessories. Now a state memorial, the five-acre estate is open free of charge year-round. Hours are 9:00 A.M. to 5:00 P.M. from Wednesday through Saturday and 1:00 to 5:00 P.M. on Tuesday and Sunday; closed Monday and major winter holidays; (812) 265–3526.

Among the other attractions in Madison's historic district are the office and private hospital of Dr. William Hutchings, with all the original medications and possessions of the late-nineteenth-century doctor still intact; a restored pioneer garden with vintage roses and other period plantings; and the Schroeder Saddle Tree Factory, now undergoing restoration, where in the last century the Schroeder family made wooden forms for horse saddles that were sold all over the world. Everywhere in Madison, you'll see elaborate ornamental ironwork reminiscent of New Orleans, but forged locally (as was much of New Orleans's ironwork). "Little Jimmy," a locally famous weathervane, sits atop the firehouse bell tower.

If the *Delta Queen,* an old sternwheeler that carries passengers on nostalgic journeys up and down the Ohio and Mississippi rivers, happens to be in port during your visit, the aura of yesteryear will be even more overwhelming.

Maps and guides for walking tours are available from the Chamber of Commerce's visitor center at 301 East Main Street, just across the street from the Jefferson County Courthouse; (812) 265–2956.

Railroad buffs will want to take a look at one of the world's steepest noncog train tracks. Cut through limestone bluffs in 1835, it climbs 413 feet in little more than a mile. Eight-horse teams drew the first trains up the incline but were eventually replaced by a wood-burning steam engine. The tracks can be viewed from State Road 56 at the west edge of town.

Madison is located in the heart of burley tobacco country, and each year from about Thanksgiving through January, auctions are conducted in local tobacco warehouses. It's a fascinating scenario, set to the music of the auctioneer's lyrical but unintelligible (to the layman) lingo. Three warehouses welcome visitors: Hughes, 748 Scott Court, (812) 273–4184; Maddox, 121 South West Street, (812) 265–3631; Morrow, 740 Clifty Drive (812) 273–3610. Check locally for varying hours.

Not far west of Madison, you can stay at the Clifty Falls State Park inn. Recently renovated, it features guest rooms for $36 per night for two; some rooms have private balconies that overlook the Ohio River valley. The dining room serves three meals a day for reasonable rates. Write Clifty Inn, Box 387, Madison 47250; (812) 265–4135.

Noted for its natural beauty, Clifty Falls State Park sprawls over 1,360 hilly acres. The prettiest area, Clifty Canyon State Nature Preserve, is accessible only on foot. The great, boulder-strewn canyon is so deep that sunlight can penetrate it only at high noon. Mosses, lichens, and ferns cling to the precipitous cliffs along Clifty Creek. In the spring, when the water is running fast, there are spectacular waterfalls; Big Clifty Falls, the granddaddy of them all, drops 60 feet. The park also offers an Olympic-size swimming pool, a modern campground, a nature center, an exercise trail and breathtaking views from atop a 400-foot bluff. Write Clifty Falls State Park, 1501 Green Rd., Madison 47250; (812) 273–5495.

Canaan is a really fowl place. In fact, there may be more fowl than people—and of more types than you ever knew existed. Schoolteacher Gale Ferris calls his poultry farm the **United Nations of the Poultry World.** Forty rare breeds populate his farmyard, including silver spangled hamburgs from Germany, black cochin bantams from Asia, bearded mottled houdans from France, and the blue-skinned Chinese silkies, as fluffy as powder puffs. The unusual araucanas from South America actually lay colored eggs.

Mr. Ferris is happy to share his wealth of knowledge—both about fowls and about Jefferson County. Early April, when all the redbuds are in bloom and baby chicks and ducks are about, is recommended. From mid-November to mid-April, it's best to come on weekends or evenings. There is no charge, but donations are appreciated. To make sure Mr. Ferris will be there when you visit, or to arrange group tours, call (812) 839–4770. The Ferris farm is located 15 miles northeast of Madison and 3 miles east of Canaan on State Road 62.

Also on the Ferris farm, housed in a little red barn, is a display of old tools and utensils dating from the early 1800s to the early 1900s, including a copper kettle, liquor jugs more than one hundred years old, and dippers for molten bullet metal. Nearby stands a miniature one-room schoolhouse that the Ferris family built from brick. It contains several pieces from an old Canaan school that was razed a few years back, including the cornerstone, coal tongs, blackboard, and school bench; other items on display are authentic antiques. Both are open to the public free of charge.

Ferris is also one of the chief organizers of Canaan's annual Fall Festival, which features a potpourri of such events as a frog jumping contest, bucksaw woodcutting contest, greased pole climbing contest, and the Chief White Eye painting contest. Held the second weekend in September, festival has become known far and wide, however, for its unique Pony Express Run. Mail is specially stamped at Canaan, packed in authentic pony express mail bags on loan from the Smithsonian Institution in Washington, D.C., and delivered to the Madison post office by a horseback rider. For further information, contact Mr. Ferris at Route 1, Canaan 47224; (812) 839–4770.

Ohio County

Rising Sun, perched on the banks of the Ohio River, exudes that "once upon a time" charm of a small town suspended in the mists of a long-ago past. Filled with historic homes and quaint shops, it also offers one of the cheapest—and nowadays rarest—boat rides anywhere. Visitors can cross the river to Rabbit Hash, Kentucky (a tourist attraction in itself), on a ferry that operates continuously from 11:00 A.M. to 5:00 P.M. on Saturday, Sunday, and holidays during summer months.

Rising Sun is also the home of **Hoosier Boy,** a hydroplane that was an internationally famous raceboat in the 1920s. You'll find it displayed in the local Ohio County Historical Museum. Each August, to celebrate its legacy, the town stages a *Hoosier Boy* Regatta.

For additional information, contact the Rising Sun/Ohio County Tourism Bureau, P.O. Box 95, Rising Sun 47040; (812) 438–2319.

Ripley County

Many a visitor, while traveling through the small town of Versailles, has stopped to stare in wonderment at the unusual-looking church on the corner of Tyson and Adams streets. Known officially as the **Tyson Methodist Church** and unofficially as the Tyson Temple, it is a continuous flow of rounded corners, arches, columns, windows, and roof. Its striking spire is a rounded, inverted cone of open-work aluminum. Inside, the altar is framed by columns that duplicate those in the Taj Mahal. The rounded ceiling above the pews is painted with the stars and constellations that appear over Indiana in October. To enhance the effect of a nighttime sky, the ceiling is illuminated by light reflected from wall fixtures. The dome over the choir loft is covered with gold leaf from Germany. Pulpit furnishings came from Italy, and the windows are from Belgium. The grand but small Tyson Church (it seats only 200 people) draws visitors from all over the nation. Free tours are offered by appointment; call (812) 689–6976 or 689–5046.

In Batesville, you can enter the old-world atmosphere of the Sherman House and enjoy some of the tastiest food in southern Indiana. Diners can select one of twenty moderately priced entrees or the specialty of the day, but fresh Maine lobster from the restaurant's tank, châteaubriand, veal cordon bleu, prime strip steaks, and Hoosier-fried chicken are among the long-time favorites. The Sherman House also offers overnight accommodations at a rate of $35–$45 for two. Although the inn has undergone several renovations since opening in 1852, the 30-inch-square, 90-foot-long yellow poplar timbers used in the original structure are still in place and still in perfect condition. Restaurant open 6:30 A.M. to 9:00 P.M. Monday through Thursday, 6:30 A.M. to 10:00

P.M. Friday and Saturday, 6:30 A.M. to 8:00 P.M. Sunday; closed Christmas and New Year's; reservations advised. Located at 35 South Main Street (State Road 229); (812) 934–2407.

Wayne County

Although it may seem an unlikely location for such an enterprise, Richmond boasts one of the largest rose-growing industries in the world. Hill Floral Products, Inc., pioneers in greenhouse rose-growing since 1881, annually ships more than 22 million cut roses to midwestern and southern states. Visitors may stroll through forty-three acres of greenhouses where more than sixty varieties of roses bloom brightly. The famed American Beauty Rose was developed here, and new hybrids continue to be produced each year.

On a free one-hour tour, you'll learn the complexities of producing a new and superior rose—the odds against doing so are about 200,000 to 1. You'll also see the special overhead conveyor belt that gently carries each individual rose to final inspection. Open 9:00 A.M. to 3:00 P.M. Monday through Friday, September through June. For tour hours, contact Hill Floral Products, Inc., 2117 Peacock Road, Richmond 47374; (317) 962–2555.

More roses bloom in Richmond's Glen Miller Park, where the Hill Memorial Rose Garden has been established in tribute to the local flower industry. The park, located on the north side of Main Street (Highway 40) just east of town, is also the site of a small zoo. Park open 6:00 A.M. to 11:00 P.M. daily.

At the **Hayes Regional Arboretum,** a 355-acre botanical preserve, you can view regional plant species—all labeled—on a 3½-mile auto tour. Also on the grounds are Indiana's first solar heated greenhouse, a fern garden, a wild bird sanctuary, 10 miles of hiking trails (one of which passes an Indian mound), and a nature center housed in a barn some 180 years old, where a telephone line permits you to eavesdrop on a colony of bees busily at work making honey. The arboretum is open 8:00 A.M. to 5:00 P.M. Tuesday through Saturday, 1:00 to 5:00 P.M. Sunday, year-round. The nature center is open 9:00 A.M. to 5:00 P.M. Tuesday through Saturday, 1:00 to 5:00 P.M. Sunday, April through November. Closed major winter holidays. Free of charge. Contact the Hayes Regional Arboretum, 801 Elks Road, Richmond 47374; (317) 962–3745.

Following a disastrous gas explosion and fire in 1968 that destroyed much of the downtown business district, Richmond covered its physical scars by building an unusual Downtown Promenade. The five blocks of flowing fountains, soft music, and unique specialty stores have been nationally acclaimed for their beauty. You'll find it on Main Street between Fifth and Tenth streets.

The Wayne County Historical Museum not far from the Promenade area is generally recognized as one of the best county museums in the state. Its diverse collection ranges from vintage cars made in Richmond to a Japanese Samurai warrior's uniform, from a nineteenth-century general store to a 3,000-year-old mummy (some x-rays of the mummy taken by two local physicians can be seen by visitors). Open 9:00 A.M. to 4:00 P.M. Tuesday through Friday and 1:00 to 4:00 P.M. Saturday and Sunday, mid-March through mid-December; closed the rest of the year and major holidays. Admission fee. Write Wayne County Historical Museum, 1150 North "A" Street, Richmond 47374; (317) 962–5756.

Although every other sport takes a back seat to basketball in Indiana, the state has also produced some football heroes. They're all honored in the Indiana Football Hall of Fame, located at the corner of North 9th and "A" streets in Richmond. Among the inductees are O. J. Simpson, Bart Starr, and Jim Thorpe, all of whom once played football in the Hoosier State; Knute Rockne, the legendary coach of Notre Dame, and Weeb Ewbank, a local great who coached the Baltimore Colts and New York Jets. Tony Hulman, whose name is synonymous with the Indianapolis 500, is remembered here as an All-American end on the undefeated Yale University team of 1923. Open 8:30 A.M. to 4:30 P.M. Monday through Friday; closed holidays. Nominal admission fee; (317) 966–2235.

Earlham College, located on the south side of Highway 40 just west of downtown Richmond, is the home of the Joseph Moore Museum of Natural Science. Such wonders as a prehistoric mastodon, an extinct giant beaver, and some authentic allosaurus skeletons are displayed, along with Ordovician fossils, arthropods, live snakes, Indiana birds of prey, and a mummy. The museum is open, free of charge, from 1:00 to 4:00 P.M. Monday, Wednesday, and Friday from September through November and January through May; also open 1:00 to 5:00 P.M. Sunday year-round and other times by appointment. A planetarium that is part of the Moore Museum presents free shows at 1:30, 2:30, and 3:30 P.M.

each Sunday. Write Earlham College, West National Road, Richmond 47374; (317) 962–6561, extensions 302/303.

Whitewater Valley Gorge Park, which borders the Whitewater River in the heart of Richmond, is one of only two known places in the United States where a unique type of limestone is exposed to the surface. Geologists, paleontologists, and amateur collectors have been coming to this site for more than a century to examine the abundance of fossils in the gorge's 425-million-year-old rock formations. The park also contains an Audubon bird sanctuary, Thistlethwaite Falls, Middlefork Reservoir, and some scenic fossil collection sites. You can obtain further information by contacting the Wayne County Convention and Tourism Bureau, 600 Promenade, Richmond, 47374; (317) 935–8687.

Centerville, about 5 miles west of Richmond on Highway 40, claims to have the greatest concentration of antique shops in the United States. **Webb's Antique Mall** alone boasts some 250 dealers. Contact the Mall's office at 200 West Union Street in Centerville; (317) 855–5542.

Fountain City is the home of the **Levi Coffin House,** known as "The Grand Central Station of the Underground Railroad." Levi and Catherine Coffin, Quakers who were opposed to slavery, opened their 1839 Federal-style home to approximately 2,000 fugitive black slaves during the Civil War era. You may know the Coffins better as Simeon and Rachel Halliday, characters in *Uncle Tom's Cabin.* Eliza Harris, the heroine of the same book, was a refugee who stayed with the Coffins for several days. The house, located on Highway 27 north, is open to the general public from 1:00 to 4:00 P.M. Tuesday through Sunday, June through mid-September; weekends only the rest of September through October; closed July 4; nominal admission fee. Write Levi Coffin House, P.O. Box 77, Fountain City 47341; (317) 847–2885.

Since Guy Welliver bought his Hagerstown restaurant in the 1940s, he has increased its seating capacity from about 50 to 500—and still customers sometimes stand in line. They do so patiently, secure in the knowledge that what awaits them is well worth it. Regular patrons include the some 2,000 lucky people who live in Hagerstown and don't have far to go, as well as diners from all over central Indiana and neighboring Ohio. What lures them is the specialty of the house—an elaborate, but reasonably priced buffet that features steamed shrimp in all-you-can-eat quantities. The homemade bread and salad bar are also highly recommended. Welliver's Smorgasbord, located at 40 East Main

Street, is open 5:00 to 8:00 P.M. Thursday, 5:00 to 9:00 P.M. Friday, 4:30 to 9:00 P.M. Saturday, and 11:00 A.M. to 8:00 P.M. Sunday (no shrimp on Sunday); (317) 489–4131.

Not far down the road from Welliver's, you can spend the night at one of the most luxurious bed-and-breakfast facilities in the Midwest. The Teetor House, a sprawling mansion built as a private home in the 1930s, is surrounded by ten acres of lawns and mature trees. Inside, you can admire the grand player piano, a staircase that duplicates those in New York City's Waldorf Astoria Hotel, a bathroom equipped with an ice-water spigot and a king-size shower with nine shower heads, stained-glass windows, rich tapestries, and polished woods. The entire estate reflects the affluence and tastes of its original owner, a self-made millionaire named Ralph Teetor who invented the speedostat (we call it cruise control today). For $55 a night per couple, guests can stay in one of four bedrooms and enjoy a breakfast served on Lenox china. Contact the Teetor House, 300 West Main Street, Hagerstown 47346; (317) 489–4422.

Just across the street, at 303 West Main Street, some thirty employees of **Tedco, Inc.,** make about 30,000 gyroscopes a month for worldwide distribution. One of the toy factory's biggest customers is the Smithsonian Institution. Five other popular toys are also produced here. Call (317) 489–5000 to arrange a free tour.

Abbott's Candy Company, the oldest continuous business in town, uses old family recipes to turn out a cornucopia of confections that are sold at a store in Hagerstown and by mail throughout the country. Its specialty and most popular sweet is the caramel, but many other varieties await visitors. Located at 48 East Walnut Street; call (317) 489–4442 for hours or to arrange a free tour.

Brian Bex has spent more than thirty years amassing the largest known collection of eagles in art. Some of his unusual pieces are exhibited at the Indianapolis Museum of Art (see listing under Marion County in Central Indiana section), but many are displayed at Mr. Bex's complex of business offices in Hagerstown. The eagles appear in a variety of forms, such as paintings and sculptures, and are made from a wide range of materials, including gold, ivory, crystal, porcelain, wood, and copper. Mr. Bex's company, American Communications, is located along State Road 1 just northeast of Hagerstown; open 8:30 A.M. to 4:30 P.M. Monday through Friday. Free guided tours, which last approximately one hour, are available by appointment; (317) 489–5566.

Off the Beaten Path in Southwest Indiana

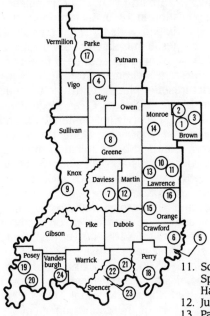

1. Brown County Art Gallery/ John Dillinger Historical Museum/Reptile Kingdom Serpentarium/Ogle Hollow State Nature Preserve
2. Possum Trot Vineyards
3. Gatesville General Store
4. Chinook Mine
5. Wyandotte Cave
6. shoe tree
7. Turkey Trot Festival
8. Worthington
9. Grouseland/Brouillet French House
10. quarries
11. Scott's Village Hardware/ Spring Mill State Park/ Hamer Pioneer Gardens
12. Jug Rock
13. Padanaram
14. Mother Bear's/Lilly Library of Rare Books and Manuscripts
15. West Baden Hotel/House of Clocks Museum
16. Punkin Center
17. Billie Creek Village
18. Tell City Pretzel Company
19. New Harmony/New Harmony Inn
20. Hovey Lake
21. St. Meinrad Benedictine Archabbey
22. Santa Claus Post Office
23. Lincoln Boyhood National Memorial
24. Wesselman Park

Southwest Indiana

Brown County

Things don't change much in Brown County. The population today is the same as the population in 1880. Each morning, the mists rise from the hills still draped with forests. Log cabins, hemmed in by split-rail fences, nestle in isolated hollows. Like as not, there's a woodpile in the yard, and on cool days fingers of wood smoke spiral up from stone chimneys. Narrow, twisting county roads lead to picturesque places with picturesque names—Gnaw Bone, Bean Blossom, Scarce O'Fat Ridge, Bear Wallow Hill, Milk-Sick Bottoms, Slippery Elm Chute Road, and Booger Holler. No billboards mar your view along the way— they're not allowed in Brown County. No air pollution muddies the landscape and offends your nostrils—Brown County has no industry. And if you're in a hurry, you're out of luck. Brown County doesn't cater to people in a hurry.

Nashville, the county seat and largest town in the county, normally has a population of about 500 people, but on October weekends that figure swells to more than 100,000. Brown County is best known for its dazzling fall color. Most folks head for Brown County State Park, some 15,000 acres of natural beauty near Nashville, but Yellowwood State Forest in western Brown County and a portion of the Hoosier National Forest that stretches across the southern part of the county offer equally spectacular and less-crowded panoramas.

In spring, Brown County is glorious with the blossoms of red-bud and dogwood trees and myriads of wildflowers. In summer, the woods offer a cool, green retreat, and for wintertime visitors, there are cross-country ski trails and a downhill ski resort.

Brown County first gained fame as a mecca for artists and craftsmen, who have been inspired by the peace and beauty of these hills since the 1870s. Today, many open their studios to the public. The Brown County Art Guild and the **Brown County Art Gallery,** both in Nashville, are among the galleries that exhibit some of their works.

Nashville is the hub of activity in Brown County—a potpourri of some 250 shops, museums, and restaurants. Craftsmen make and sell quilts, pottery, wood carvings, metal sculptures, hand-carved candles, leather goods, silver and gold jewelry made to order, stained glass wares, doll houses, handblown art glass, dulcimers, and much more. At many shops, you can watch the craftsmen at work.

Other antique shops in the area are more elegant. Just southwest of Nashville is Alberts' Mall, where Patti and Keith Albert have arranged 22 rooms of antiques in beautiful home settings; (812) 988–2397. One of the loveliest shops in Nashville is Michael's Antiques and Dried Flowers, where Mike and Cyd Nickels sell items that harmonize with log cabins (Mike will also build you a log cabin anywhere in Brown County) and the largest selection of dried flowers in the Midwest; (812) 988–7763.

Indiana is John Dillinger territory—he was born in Mooresville, and it's believed that he buried much of his still-unrecovered loot from bank robberies in various parts of the Hoosier State. Local oldtimers still relate how James Jenkins, a member of Dillinger's gang, was gunned down in Bean Blossom, just north of Nashville, after a jailbreak. The **John Dillinger Historical Museum** located on the southwest corner of Franklin and Van Buren streets in Nashville houses about 95 percent of all known publicly displayed memorabilia of one of this country's most infamous criminals. Among the exhibits are the original tombstone from Dillinger's Indianapolis grave (see Marion County in central Indiana), bank robbery plans written in Dillinger's own hand, the carved wooden pistol he used to escape from a northern Indiana jail (see Lake County in northwestern Indiana), and a vintage Ford Motor Company ad that asks: "Will they catch Dillinger? Not until they get him out of a Ford V-8!" An upstairs room is a recreation of the funeral parlor in which the notorious gangster was laid out, complete with a wax likeness of Dillinger in a coffin. Open daily, 10:00 A.M. to 6:00 P.M., March through November; irregular hours during the rest of the year. Admission fee; (812) 988–7172.

A block east of the Dillinger Museum is the **Reptile Kingdom Serpentarium.** Owner Tom Tilton, who has collected more than 200 specimens from every continent except Australia (where exports of reptiles are forbidden), says his place "crawls with excitement"—and with giant pythons, cobras, gila monsters, green anacondas, alligator snapping turtles and a green mamba. Tom also has some monkeys, which have occasionally escaped from their communal cage. Being shy creatures, they take to the town's roofs and treetops and delight human onlookers with their antics. Tom has been known to put baby boa constrictors up for adoption, but only if you can prove that you'll provide a good home for them. Open 10:30 A.M. to 7:00 P.M. daily, March through November; weekends during the rest of the year. Admission fee; (812) 988–4645.

With no seat more than 11 rows from the stage, the Brown County Playhouse in Nashville doesn't have a bad seat in the house. Performers are from the Theatre and Drama Department at Indiana University in Bloomington. Shows are at 8:00 P.M. Friday and Saturday nights during summer and fall weekends. Admission fee. For information and advance tickets, contact Indiana University Auditorium, Bloomington 47405; (812) 335–1103. In season, you may also call the Playhouse at (812) 988–2123 from 1:00 to 4:00 P.M. daily and after 5:00 P.M. on evenings of performances.

A complex of authentic nineteenth-century buildings just northeast of the courthouse in Nashville is known collectively as the Country Museum. Carding, spinning, and weaving are demonstrated in an old log barn that now serves as headquarters for the Brown County Historical Society; (812) 988–2526. You'll also see a country doctor's office, a blacksmith's shop and a log cabin home, all complete with furnishings, and an unusual log jail that claims the distinction of being the only jail in the state that ever permitted a prisoner to be his own keeper. While serving a sentence for bootlegging, the prisoner went wherever he wanted to during the day, locked himself up at night, acted as a guide for tourists, and once aided the sheriff in making an arrest. Open 1:00 to 5:00 P.M. Saturdays, Sundays, and holidays, May through October. Admission fee. The buildings can always be viewed, however, from the outside.

Just east of Nashville on State Road 46 is the northern entrance to Brown County State Park, accessible via Indiana's only divided, two-lane covered bridge (c. 1838). Enjoy 27 miles of scenic roads, hiking and bridle trails, a nature center, campgrounds (including one for horsemen), an archery range, an Olympic-size swimming pool, a lodge with a restaurant and rustic rental cabins. A nature trail leads through **Ogle Hollow State Nature Preserve,** noteworthy for its rare yellowwood trees. Open year-round during daylight hours; vehicle entrance fee April through October. Write Brown County State Park, Box 25, Nashville 47448;

(812) 988–7316. For lodge and cabin reservations, write Abe Martin Lodge, Box 25, Nashville 47448; (812) 988–7316.

Continuing east from the park on State Road 46, you'll come to State Road 135, which leads south into a secluded and little-known part of Brown County. Follow State Road 135 to an area known locally as Stone Head, so called because of the unique monument by the side of the highway that serves as a road sign—a white stone head atop a stone pillar. Every once in a while, a prankster makes off with the carving, but an outraged community has always managed to recover it.

Proceed on State Road 135 to the tiny community of Story, where a decaying feed mill and a few other tumbledown buildings bear mute testimony to old dreams. Several attempts have been made to restore the town as a tourist attraction, but all such efforts thus far have been abandoned. The Story Inn and Restaurant, however, is open for brunch from 8:00 A.M. to 2:00 P.M. each Saturday and Sunday, as well as for private dinners by advance reservation; (812) 988–2273 evenings and weekends.

Back on State Road 46, about 4 miles east of Nashville, is the hamlet of Gnaw Bone. In late summer and autumn, you can find your way there by following the tantalizing scents. That's when the area's sugar cane is pressed down into sap at a horse-driven mill, then boiled down to molasses at the Brown County Sorghum Mill. You can purchase the sorghum, persimmon pudding, cob honey, sorghum cakes, persimmon and black walnut fudge, apple butter and cider—by the gallon or glass. Hours may vary, but are usually 8:00 A.M. to sunset daily, September through November.

At Helmsburg, on State Road 45 in northwestern Brown County, a small factory near the railroad tracks houses the Cullum Broom & Mop Co. The decor and machinery belong to an early twentieth-century era. Owner James Cullum and a handful of employees make sturdy corn brooms and mops before your eyes. Visitors are welcome 8:00 A.M. to 3:00 P.M. Monday through Friday. Write Cullum Broom and Mop Co., Helmsburg 47435; (812) 988–4897.

Ben and Lee Sparks, owners of the **Possum Trot Vineyards,** welcome visitors to their mom-and-pop winery west of Trevlac. The Sparkses claim to give the "most informative winery tour in the United States." It's also one of the friendliest. Two of their specialty products, Zaraqueya Sangria and mulled wine, are state fair prize winners. Open for drop-in visits and tours, complete with wine tasting, from 10:00 A.M. to 6:00 P.M. (or sunset, if earlier); Sunday, noon to 6:00 P.M. mid-March to mid-December, and by appointment at other times. Nominal fee for tour. Located near the north shore of Lake Lemon in northwestern Brown County. Hiking, rockhounding, and picnicking are permitted on the grounds. Write Possum Trot Vineyards, 8310 North Possum Trot Rd., Unionville 47468; (812) 988-2694.

Gold has been mined on a small scale in Brown County since the mid-1800s, and you can still pan for it at several locations along Salt Creek. At the **Gatesville General Store,** on the banks of Salt Creek in northeastern Brown County, you can purchase a gold pan and try your luck right outside the door. The store also claims to sell the largest homemade sandwiches in the area, featuring more than 100 combinations. To wash them down, there's fresh-squeezed lemonade. Open 9:00 A.M. to 7:00 P.M. Monday through Saturday, 1:00 to 5:00 P.M. Sunday; closed Christmas and New Year's Day; (812) 988-0477.

Brown County's hills are just that—hills. The highest point in the county is 1,489 feet above sea level, but there's still a respectable downhill ski area on State Road 46 southwest of Nashville that offers all the makings for a fine winter holiday—seven slopes and trails with a vertical drop of 250 feet, a bunny slope for beginners, chair lifts, rope tows, a lodge, ski shop and dining facilities. Ski World also hosts many activities during the annual Brown County Winter Festival, held in early February. Open 10:00 A.M. to 10:00 P.M. Monday through Thursday, 8:00 A.M. to midnight Friday through Sunday and holidays, mid-December to early March (weather permitting); closed Christmas Eve. Write Ski World, Box 445, Nashville 47448; (812) 988-6638 or 988-6693.

Tourists, as well as armies, travel on their stomachs. The most popular of the many fine eateries in Nashville is the Nashville House, located on the corner of Main and Van Buren streets in the center of town. Its charming rustic atmosphere is enhanced by antique furniture, checkered tablecloths, and a huge stone fireplace. The dinner menu lists such Hoosier favorites as fried ham steak, baked ham, barbecue ribs, roast turkey and country fried chicken, but the highlight of any meal has to be the fried biscuits. These delicious deep-fried dough balls, served with baked apple butter, could make an addict of anyone. Owner Andy Rogers says they were invented by his father, Jack Rogers, around 1947. The Nashville House is no place for dieters—not only is everything sinfully fattening, but unless you're a lumberjack, you might be hard put to eat everything that's put in front of you. Although the menu is limited, the food is country cooking at its finest. Prices range from $12.65 to $15.85 for dinner; children's plates are half price. Open 11:30 A.M. to 8:00 P.M., daily in October and daily except Tuesday the rest of the year; closed for two weeks during the Christmas season. Reservations are accepted except during October; (812) 988–4554.

The entrance to the Nashville House is through the Old Country Store, a pleasant place to browse if you have to wait for seating in the restaurant. It's just what the name implies—a delightful clutter of goods that includes many hard-to-find items from yesteryear.

Anyone with a sweet tooth should head for The Candy Store, just west of the Nashville post office, where you can indulge in more than 500 varieties of domestic and imported candies and other fine foods. Licorice-lovers from as far away as California drop in here, having heard by word-of-mouth about a small store in Nashville, Indiana, that stocks an average of over 100 varieties of licorice. Much of the candy is made on the premises, and mail order service is provided to almost anywhere in the world. Open 9:00 A.M. to 5:00 P.M. year-round. Closed Thanksgiving and Christmas. Write The Candy Store, Box 364, Nashville 47448; (812) 988–2028.

Need a cup of hot brew and a pleasant corner in which to relax a spell? Drop in at The Daily Grind. You'll find it in Nashville's Calvin Place, a cluster of shops behind the John Dillinger Museum. Although coffee houses have dropped from the scene in many places, this one is alive and well, thank you. No one gets sticky about it, but from the moment you lift the latch and walk through the heavy wooden door, you feel welcome here. Your main problem will be making a decision. There are nearly twenty different gourmet coffees from all over the world and fifty varieties of tea—all served in stoneware mugs. Go-withs include a salad bar, sandwiches, soup, potato salad, and pastries. Stored on the mantel of the stone fireplace is a selection of such games as chess, checkers, and backgammon—help yourself. Read one of the newspapers lying about or play a game of darts. The country store area offers coffee beans, apothecary jars filled with tea leaves, coffee mugs, spices, tea pots, and coffee makers. The Daily Grind, which fills mail orders, is open year round; 9:00 A.M. to 10:00 P.M. daily. Live entertainment is featured Saturday nights.

Hours may vary in the winter. Write The Daily Grind, Box 607, Nashville 47448; (812) 988–4808.

Overnight facilities in and near Nashville range from resort inns to motels, from bed-and-breakfast rooms in private homes to furnished log cabins with equipped kitchens. Many are booked up as much as two years in advance, especially on weekends from spring through fall and the week before Christmas, so plan ahead. For more information, contact the Brown County Convention & Vistors Bureau, Franklin House, Nashville 47448; (812) 988–7303.

While in Nashville, buy a copy of the Brown County Democrat, which has been honored as Indiana's finest weekly newspaper more times than anyone can remember. The "Sheriff's Log" therein is a Brown County classic. Some recent entries read thus:

> *Man called and said he just put on a pot of coffee if any officers are in the area and want coffee.*
> *Girl at restaurant requests a conservation officer.*
> *An owl is sitting on the pizza oven.*
> *Trouble reported at the city dump. Someone abandoned a person there.*
> *A coon is asleep on the shelf (of a local shop) with a teddy bear.*
> *Man wants deputy (any deputy) to meet him so that he can borrow $5 or $10.*
> *Man requests Nashville town marshal go to restaurant and check the stove to see if he left a pot of beans on.*

Like the mythical sheriff's office in Mayberry, N.C., made famous by a television series, this one's run with a lot of heart.

Clay County

Some of Indiana's richest coal reserves can be seen in the strip mines that line the roadside near Brazil. Known as the Brazil Block district because the coal usually breaks into nearly perfect rectangular blocks, the region first became a center for bituminous coal production in the 1850s. Once strip mining left desolate scars on the earth; today, with increased environmental awareness, these areas are no longer being exploited and then abandoned. Vegetation is planted to prevent erosion, and pit holes become recreational lakes that offer swimming, boating, and fishing.

The Amax Coal Co., third largest coal producer in the United States and one of the most environmentally aware, gives free guided tours of its **Chinook Mine** near Brazil. You must, however, give them a minimum of two weeks' advance notice. Tour groups are made up of eight to sixteen persons, and participants must be at least twelve years old. Contact the Brazil Chamber of Commerce, (812) 448–8457 or Amax Coal Co., (Indianapolis), (317) 266–1500.

While in the area, enjoy the excellent buffet served at Adami's Restaurant on Highway 40 about 5 miles west of Brazil. You won't see many advertisements for Adami's—owners Max and Betty Bayard believe in putting their money where everyone's mouth is. Good food and satisfied customers spread the word. The seafood buffet, served on Thursday nights, is touted as the finest in the Midwest; prices, generally, are in the moderate range (about $9–$11), with special prices for children under ten. Open 5:00 to 9:00 P.M. Wednesday through Saturday, noon to 7:00 P.M. Sunday; (812) 446–3241.

Crawford County

Most spelunkers are aware of the subterranean wonders that exist in the Hoosier state, but few other people know that there is a proliferation of caves in southern Indiana. Several of those open to the public are in Crawford County.

Thanks to being mentioned in both Ripley's "Believe It or Not" column and the *Guinness Book of World Records,* **Wyandotte Cave** has become world famous for its Monument Mountain—the highest underground mountain in any known cave on earth. It stands 135 feet tall, the focal point of an awe-inspiring room known as Rothrock's Cathedral, which is approximately 185 feet high, 360 feet long and 140 feet wide. Your tour guide may introduce you to the ghost of Chief Wyandotte, a weird and entertaining play of shadows at the top of the Cathedral. Superlatives apply elsewhere in the cave, too: a room half a mile in circumference and 200 feet high is the largest subterranean room known anywhere in the world, and a resplendent stalagmite 35 feet high and 75 feet around is believed to be the world's largest formation of its kind. With some 25 miles of known passages explored, the cave itself is among earth's largest. You'll also see delicate and exquisite formations called helictites that are extremely rare. A two-hour walk covers 1 1/2 miles; if you're the rugged type, opt for a five- or eight-hour tour during which you'll not only walk, but crawl, climb, descend a pole once used by Indians and, in places, travel by lantern light.

Just south of Wyandotte Cave is Little Wyandotte Cave, which can be toured in about thirty minutes. This cave is much more ordinary, but enjoyable for those who've never been in a cavern before.

To reach the caves, travel west from Corydon on State Road 62 for about 12 miles and turn north on a blacktop road; signs point the way. Admission fees; advance reservations necessary for the five-hour and eight-hour tours. Although available all year, tours are conducted more frequently in the summer. Nature provides a constant temperature of 52 degrees all year long for both caves. Open Memorial Day to Labor Day 9:00 A.M.–6:00 P.M., Labor Day to Memorial Day 8:00 A.M.–5:00 P.M.; closed Mondays. Write Wyandotte Caves, Route 1, Box 60A, Leavenworth, 47137; (812) 738–2782.

The state-owned caves are part of a larger recreation area known as the Harrison-Crawford Wyandotte Complex. Besides the caves, it includes the Wyandotte Woods State Recreation Area and the Harrison-Crawford State Forest, both of which straddle the Harrison-Crawford county line. Wyandotte Woods offers developed campsites, hiking and bridle trails, a nature center, views of the Ohio River, and an Olympic size swimming pool. For those who enjoy roughing it, Harrison-Crawford State Forest has primitive campsites and overnight backpacking trails. To reach both, travel west from Corydon on State Road 62 for about 8 miles to State Road 462 and turn south; State Road 462 runs through the forest and ends in Wyandotte Woods. For information on both the forest and the recreation area, contact Harrison-Crawford State Forest, 7240 Old Forest Road, Corydon 47112; (812) 738–8232.

Not far north of Wyandotte Caves is Marengo Cave, discovered in 1883 by a young brother and sister exploring a sinkhole. The cave, a comfortable 54 degrees at all times, has been open to the public ever since, and its beauty has been acclaimed throughout the world. Concerts were once held in a subterranean room noted for its acoustics, and an early-day evangelist preached his fiery message from Pulpit Rock. Underground weddings and dances were regular occurrences throughout the years, and a square dance is still held in the Music Hall Chamber each July.

Two tours are offered. The highlight of the ¹/₃-mile tour is Crystal Palace, acknowledged by speleologists as one of the ten most beautiful cavern rooms anywhere. A 1-mile tour through a different part of the cave features totem pole stalagmites and a cavern passage big enough to build a highway through. Above the cavern is a 112-acre park, complete with campsites and trail rides atop horses from the park's stables. Separate fee for each tour, special combination price for both. Cave open daily, year-round, except Thanksgiving and Christmas; Memorial Day to Labor Day 9:00 A.M. to 6:00 P.M. and Labor Day to Memorial Day 9:00 A.M. to 5:00 P.M. Marengo Cave is just northeast of the town of Marengo; go east from Marengo on State Road 64/66 and follow the signs. Write Marengo Cave Park, Box 217, Marengo 47140; (812) 365-2705.

Twisting its way southward through Crawford County is the lovely, spring-fed Blue River, Indiana's first officially designated natural and scenic river and an ideal canoe stream. Several outfitters offer trips, ranging from 7 to 58 miles in length; on longer trips, you spend the night on the river. Depending on the trip you take, you'll float quiet waters and shoot rapids, pass caves, springs, limestone bluffs, and walls of trees; make your way around rock gardens and through narrow gorges. The fishing is some of the best in the Midwest, producing catches of bass, crappie, bluegill, and catfish; and the serenity can be well nigh incredible. In its lower stretches, just before it joins the Ohio, the Blue River turns sluggish—perfect for tubing. Rates for canoeing range from $7.50–$21 per person and include paddle, life jacket and shuttle service; special rates for children. The season is usually April through October, but water levels are best for canoeing before mid-July. Contact the Clark/Floyd/Harrison Counties Convention and Visitors Bureau, P.O. Box 608, Jeffersonville 47131 (812) 282-6654, for names of outfitters in the area.

About 5 miles south of Milltown is one of southern Indiana's most curious landmarks—a white oak known locally as the **"shoe tree."** Most days, more than 150 pairs of shoes of all shapes, sizes, and colors can be seen dangling from its branches. No one seems to know exactly when the custom started, but it dates back at least 25 years. Local folks speculate that someone thought of his shoes as long-time friends that had served him faithfully and well and deserved a better fate than to be uncere-

111

moniously dumped in the garbage, so he decided to inter them in a permanent place of honor. Inquire in Milltown for directions; the tree stands at the junction of two gravel roads that aren't shown on any map.

Just west of Milltown, on the north side of State Road 64, is an old limestone quarry with an intriguing maze of tunnels dug into the side of a hill. Inside the cavernous excavations, eerie echoes bombard your ears—the flutter of birds' wings, dripping water, your own footsteps. Ceilings at least 20 feet high, supported by great stone buttresses, and the silent halls they enclose create the impression that you are entering some ancient catacombs or perhaps a cathedral, now hushed and still, whose days of glory have been lost in the mists of time. Explore at your own risk.

The little town of Leavenworth on the Ohio River likens its history to that of Noah and the ark—the oldest establishments in town date back to just after the flood. The granddaddy of all floods on the Ohio occurred in 1937, and most of the riverside town of Leavenworth was washed away to points south. Undaunted, residents moved up to a blufftop and started over. Lack of money, like politics, can make for strange bedfellows, so a small cafe and a grocery store shared the second floor of a chicken hatchery. From those humble beginnings has evolved a family restaurant called The Overlook, which now occupies the entire building. Through the years, the restaurant has specialized in good home cooking and reasonable prices, and people go out of their way to stop here. Even if the food weren't so good, it would be worth stopping at The Overlook just for the view—a sweeping panorama of forested hills and the broad Ohio River as it arches around a horseshoe bend. Outside stands what is believed to be the largest redbud tree in the world. The Overlook, located on the south side of State Road 62 in Leavenworth, is open daily, year-round, except Christmas, for breakfast, lunch, and dinner; 8:00 A.M. to 10:00 P.M. Monday through Saturday, 8:00 A.M. to 9:00 P.M. Sundays and holidays, April through October; 9:00 A.M. to 9:00 P.M., November through March. Dinner prices range from $7–$16. Write Box 85, Leavenworth 47137; (812) 739–4264.

Not far northwest of Leavenworth are the White Oaks Country Cabins, which nestle in the midst of the Hoosier National Forest near Patoka Lake, one of Indiana's newest water playgrounds. No two cottages in this peaceful spot are alike. One, for instance, is a restored 150-year-old log home, while another has been converted from a barn. The cabins accommodate from two to four people each, with additional cots available. Each is fully equipped, including linens and cookware. Contact Jack and Juanita Brown, White Oaks Country Cabins, RR 1, Taswell 47175; (812) 338-3085. The cabins lie north of State Road 64 near Taswell; the Browns will give you exact directions when you make your reservations.

Daviess County

Along about 1972, the local folks decided they needed a unique attraction to put Daviess County on the map, and their idea brought them fame that exceeded their wildest expectations. They combined Indiana's best known event, the Indianapolis 500 Race, with Daviess County's best known product, turkeys, and gave birth to the **Turkey Trot Festival.**

Come mid-September, turkeydom's finest make their way to Ruritan Park in Montgomery for four days of the most laughable racing imaginable. Because there are about 40 turkeys to every human in Daviess County (with a noticeable but temporary change in the ratio just after the Thanksgiving and Christmas holidays), there can be a lot of birds to face off. This requires many preliminary heats, and only the cream of the crop survive the grueling schedule to race in the final championship run.

On the last, fateful day, anxious jockeys lead their tethered birds to the starting line, eager to put weeks of training to the test. Some raw talent is always on hand, too, since many owners believe that training a bird with a brain the size of a man's thumbnail is a waste of time. Onlookers cheer their personal favorites—such racing greats as Dirty Bird, White Lightning, and Turkey Lurkey.

On signal, the turkeys head down a 213-foot-long straightaway track toward a finish line that, for a top turkey trotter, is approximately twenty seconds away. Alas, prima donnas are inevitable. Some refuse to start at all. The more befuddled go sideways or backwards. Still others tire along the way and pause to peck at whatever turkeys like to peck at. Some even take to the air, disdainfully rising above it all. Eventually, however, one galloping gobbler manages to cross the finish line and is declared the grand champion.

Another big event is the best dressed turkey contest, which inspires elaborate costumes. One recent winner devastated the

judges when she modeled her stunning powder blue bikini, then
further charmed them by coyly batting her false eyelashes.

And if you think they don't take all this seriously in Daviess
County, consider the fact that these are the only turkey races in
the world sanctioned by the National Turkey Federation. The
races have received national attention from the day of their in-
ception, and stories about them have been translated into five
foreign languages and printed all around the globe. Spectators
come from all over the United States.

Although the turkeys are obviously the main attraction, the
festival also features tractor pulls and entertainment by top country music stars. For additional information, contact Russ Titzer,
Green Acres, Loogootee 47553, (812) 254–3363.

Greene County

No matter what you've read or been told, there is no way to
fully prepare you for your first glimpse of the Greene County
viaduct. One minute you're driving along an isolated rural road
that winds through wooded hills and hollows. The next minute
you're suddenly confronted with an open valley and the massive
railroad trestle that spans it. It is one of the most spectacular
sights in the state.

Completed in 1906 as part of the Illinois Central Railroad line,
the viaduct is 180 feet high and 2,295 feet long—the second longest in the world. (To see the longest, you'll have to travel to Can-
tal, France.) Park beneath the massive steel girders that support it,
and climb a well-worn path up the hill at the north end for a
sweeping view.

The viaduct is located just south of a road that links Solsberry
and the hamlet of Tulip. Head west from Solsberry on the country
road that parallels the railroad tracks. After driving about 5 miles,
you'll come to County Road 480E, which turns off to the south
and leads beneath the trestle.

It's best to stop at the general store in Solsberry and ask for
exact directions. Roads are not well marked hereabouts, and besides, it's great fun to listen to the yarns being spun by any occupants of the store's "liars' bench." Maybe they'll tell you the one
about the man wearing gum rubber boots who fell off the viaduct
while it was being constructed and bounced for three days. He
finally had to be shot to keep him from starving to death. For

additional information, contact the Bloomfield Chamber of Commerce, P.O. Box 144, Bloomfield 47424; (812) 384–3575.

In the vast, dense forest that covered most of Indiana during the last century, there grew a sycamore that was the largest tree in the eastern half of the United States. Naturalists and historians advised everyone to go to **Worthington** and see this wonderful tree, which stood 150 feet high, spread its branches to a length of 100 feet, and measured more than 42 feet in circumference at 5 feet above the ground.

In 1920, a storm toppled it, and the town of Worthington decided to preserve one of its limbs in a place of honor. That limb, more than 23 feet in circumference and larger than the trunks of most trees in Indiana today, may be seen in Worthington's City Park at the north end of town. You can't miss it—it's the only tree in the park with a roof over its head. The Worthington Chamber of Commerce (c/o Ferris Trading Post, 310 Third St., Worthington 47471; (812) 875–3657) can tell you more about it.

Knox County

Vincennes, Indiana's oldest city, has a colorful history, and the town abounds with monuments to its past. George Rogers Clark came here during the American Revolution to battle the Indians, and his deeds are memorialized in the George Rogers Clark National Historical Park, located at 401 South Second St. (open 9:00 A.M. to 5:00 P.M. daily; free). Within a magnificent round stone structure are seven murals depicting Clark's campaigns.

In Harrison Historical Park, near the corner of First and Scott streets on the western edge of Vincennes University campus, is a two-story white frame building that served as the capitol for the Indiana Territory until 1813. Nearby is the Western Sun Print Shop where the territory's first newspaper was published on July 4, 1804. Legend has it that Abe Lincoln, a faithful reader of the *Sun*, came here as a young man to study a printing press in operation and actually helped print the Saturday, March 6, 1830, edition of the paper on the day of his visit. Both sites may be seen for one admission fee; open 9:30 A.M. to 4:30 P.M. Tuesday through Saturday; noon to 4:30 P.M. Sunday, from Easter through Thanksgiving.

Also in the park is **Grouseland,** an early nineteenth-century Georgian mansion that was the home of William Henry Harrison when he served as the first governor of the Indiana Territory (he later became the ninth President of the United States and was grandfather of the twenty-third). As part of his official duties, he once invited Indian Chief Tecumseh to his home to discuss their differences. Tecumseh refused to come inside, saying that he preferred to sit on the earth, his mother, and so the two men held council in a walnut grove on the front lawn. (Open daily, 9:00 A.M. to 5:00 P.M. March through December, except Thanksgiving and Christmas; 11:00 A.M. to 4:00 P.M. January through February, except New Year's Day; admission fee.) The boundaries of the Indiana Territory first encompassed the present-day states of Indiana, Illinois, Michigan, Wisconsin, part of Minnesota and later the lands included in the 1803 Louisiana Purchase, so tiny Vincennes, with Harrison at its helm, was for a while the seat of government for most of America from the Alleghenies to the Rockies.

Harrison also served as one of the first trustees of Vincennes University; founded in 1801, it is the oldest university west of the Alleghenies.

St. Francis Xavier Cathedral (207 Church St.), dating back to 1702, is the oldest Catholic church in Indiana. The present red brick building is actually the fourth church to stand on this site; its first two predecessors were built of logs, while the third, also a brick structure, was built in 1826 and rebuilt later the same year after a storm nearly destroyed it. Rich, dark cedars shelter the serene grounds of the Old French Cemetery adjacent to the Cathedral, where priests, laymen, Indians, soldiers, and Negro slaves lie buried, many in unmarked graves. The first interment was in 1741, the last in 1846.

Behind the cathedral, housed in a modern red brick building, is Brute Library, the oldest library in Indiana, containing more than 11,000 rare books and documents. Bishop Simon Brute (1779–1839), the First Bishop of Vincennes, who assembled the collection in France and brought it with him to the wilderness that was the Indiana Territory, was called by President John Quincy Adams "the most learned man of his day in America."

A papal bull of Pope John XXII, dated 1319 and written on heavy parchment, is the oldest manuscript. The oldest book, dated 1476, glows with the lustrous colors of hand illumination, and the parchment still bears the holes made by the pins that held the pages in place while the illuminating was done. Another interesting volume contains the Lord's Prayer in 250 different languages. In addition, there are old maps, letters and a certified

Grouseland

copy of a license issued on March 6, 1833, to Abraham Lincoln and William Berry, permitting them to operate a tavern in New Salem, Ill. The library and cathedral are open 9:00 A.M. to 5:00 P.M. daily (the library occasionally closes during winter months).

Built around 1806, the **Brouillet French House** at 509 North First St. is one of six remaining upright log and mud houses in North America. Inside are the original fireplace and warming oven, along with authentic period furnishings. Open 1:00 to 4:00 P.M. daily, June through September; admission fee.

All these attractions and others lie along Vincennes' "Mile of History" on or near the banks of the Wabash River. Tickets for the Trailblazer Tour, a forty-minute narrated excursion aboard an open-air bus, may be purchased at the Log Cabin Visitors' Center in Harrison Historical Park. The train operates from Easter through November; hours vary. (812) 885–4339.

A remnant of prehistory, the Sonotabac Indian Mound (2401 Wabash Ave.) was constructed around 300 B.C. You can journey even further back in time within the museum at the mound's base, where exhibits and artifacts date back to 8,000 B.C. Admission fee. Open daily, 10:00 A.M. to 4:00 P.M., Sunday 1:00 to 4:00 P.M., May through September, and weekends in October. (812) 882–7679. Several other Indian mounds lie to the east and south of Vincennes.

Red Skelton, the beloved comedian, was born in Vincennes at 111 West Lyndale Ave. A sign in front of the house commemorates the occasion. When Red was just ten years old, he joined the Hagenbach and Wallace Circus (which wintered in Peru, IN) as a clown.

The famed Gimbel's Department Store chain also claims Vincennes as its home. Ed Gimbel and his seven sons opened their first store here at the corner of Second and Water streets.

For additional information, contact the Knox County Chamber of Commerce, 417 Busseron St., P.O. Box 553, Vincennes 47591; (812) 882–6440.

Lawrence County

For more than 100 years, many of the great public edifices in this country have been constructed with Indiana limestone. Architects favor it because it lends itself easily to carving and the most delicate tracery when first quarried, then becomes hard and durable when exposed to atmospheric agents. The Empire State Building (it withstood King Kong, you know) and Rockefeller Center in New York City, Washington Cathedral, the Pentagon and Chicago's Merchandise Mart are just a few of the structures that are built at least partially of oolitic limestone (so called because of its granular composition, which suggests a mass of fish eggs) from the Bedford area.

The **quarries** are quite impressive to see—great, gaping cavities in the earth from which are extracted immense blocks of stone that average 4 feet in thickness, 10 feet in width, and from 50 to 100 feet in length. Before being removed from the quarry floor, they're broken into small blocks for easy transportation to a processing mill. To view the quarries, go north from Bedford on State Road 37 through Oolitic; the quarries are about one-half mile north of Oolitic.

When you pass through Oolitic, stop and meet a new town resident—a limestone statue of Joe Palooka, which stands in front of the town hall. A famous comic strip character from out of the not-too-distant past, Joe was at the peak of his popularity in the 1940s (although it's rumored that he may be making a comeback via a television cartoon). A paragon of good, Joe was an earthbound Superman of sorts who championed democracy and decency and was an inspiration to the youth of his day. He was also a boxer, and he is depicted—10 feet tall and weighing more than ten tons—wearing trunks and boxing gloves.

About five years ago, the Bedford Industrial Development Foundation, a nonprofit financial arm of the Chamber of Commerce, opened a twenty-acre limestone demonstration center, which overlooks the two largest quarries. A museum was built, displays of machinery and tools were set up, and construction was begun on the two main attractions—a $1/5$-scale limestone replica of the Great Pyramid of Cheops and a 650-foot duplication of a segment from the Great Wall of China. At this writing, the project is at a standstill because of a lack of funds, but the Chamber hopes to reopen it in the near future. For an update, contact the Bedford Chamber of Commerce, 2999 West 16th St., Box 68, Bedford 47421; (812) 275–4493.

Bedford stone, another name for local limestone, is sometimes used for gravestones, and many fine examples can be seen in Green Hill Cemetery, 1202 Eighteenth St., Bedford. The monument for Louis Baker, a 23-year-old apprentice stonecutter who died suddenly in 1917, was carved by his grieving fellow workers;

119

they reproduced his workbench, fully detailed even to actual size, exactly as he had left it for the last time. Still another marker is a life-sized statue of Tom Bardon, who died while playing golf in 1937; he's proudly and eternally clutching a bag full of golf clubs.

If you feel the need for refreshment while in Bedford, stop in at **Scott's Village Hardware** (that's right—hardware!) on the east side of the square at 1516 I St. The piece de resistance is the authentic ice cream soda, a frothy delight served up in the tall, frosted, fluted, footed glasses of yesteryear. Chocolate and strawberry are the most popular flavors, but you can also choose vanilla, pineapple, cherry, orange, or lemon.

At Purdue University's Feldun Purdue Agricultural Center, you can roam the 449 acres of the Moses Fell Farm. Mr. Fell donated the farm to Purdue University in 1914, and it has been used ever since for experimental purposes. Located on State Road 158 4 miles west of Bedford; signs point the way. Open daily, year-round; 6:30 A.M. to 5:30 P.M. Monday through Saturday; 6:30 A.M. to 4:00 P.M. Sunday; free admission. Feldun Purdue Agricultural Center, Dar Hollow Rd., Bedford 47421; (812) 275–6756.

Southwest of Bedford, our country's longest "lost river" flows through a startling subterranean world. Twenty miles of passageways have currently been explored at Bluespring Caverns, one of the world's ten longest, and most of those miles are wet ones— inundated by a system of underground streams. Visitors descend a stairway into the sinkhole entrance room, then venture 4,000 feet into the yawning depths aboard flat-bottomed boats that glide silently through a world of total darkness. The rare white fish and crayfish that live in these waters are blind, having adapted themselves over the years to a habitat where sight is of no use. Lights mounted on the bottom of the tour boat create shifting shadows on fluted walls and provide unique glimpses of water-sculpted formations on the mirror-like surface of the stream. By prior arrangement, you can also participate in a "wild tour," which includes exploration of some of the dry portions of the cave, crawling, climbing and an underground slide show.

This is one place where weather will never surprise you—the temperature is a constant 52 degrees year-round. To reach Bluespring Caverns Park from Bedford, go south on U.S. 50 for about 6 miles, then turn northwest on Stumphole Bridge Rd. for about half a mile; signs point the way. Open 9:00 A.M. to 6:00 P.M. daily, May through September; Saturday and Sunday, April and October. Last tour leaves at 5:00 P.M. Admission fee. Campsites with water and electricity are available in the park. Bluespring Caverns Park, RR 11, Box 479, Bedford 47421; (812) 279–9892.

The many attractions at **Spring Mill State Park** span a time period from the early 1800s to the threshold of the space age. As a boy growing up in nearby Mitchell, Virgil I. (Gus) Grissom loved this park. Grissom grew up to become one of the seven original astronauts and, in 1965, the second American in space. Two years later, he was dead—one of three astronauts killed in a tragic spacecraft fire at Cape Kennedy. The Gemini III capsule in which he made his historic flight now rests, along with his space suit and other items related to space travel, in the Grissom Memorial Visitor Center. Open daily, year-round.

Nestled in a small valley among the park's wooded hills is a pioneer village that was founded in 1814. Its sawmill, meeting house, apothecary, hatmaker's and weaver's shops, water-powered gristmill, general store, tavern, distillery, post office, and log cabin homes have all been restored, and from April through October, they are alive with inhabitants who go about their daily routine just as their long-ago counterparts did. You may purchase cornmeal ground at the old gristmill and products from the weaver's looms, and, on occasion, you can participate in candlelight tours of the tiny settlement.

Plants in the **Hamer Pioneer Gardens** are the same as those grown by the village's original occupants; some were used for medicine, some for cooking and some simply to add beauty to a life that was often harsh. Uphill from the village is a pioneer cemetery that dates back to 1832. The stone markers provide a genealogical history of the town below.

During the spring and summer, nearly every variety of wildflower and bird indigenous to Indiana is found here, and to protect some of the 1,300-acre park's finest natural features, the state has set aside two areas as nature preserves. A 2$\frac{1}{2}$-mile loop hiking trail, the most beautiful in the park, winds through the Donaldson Woods Nature Preserve, an outstanding 76-acre virgin forest dominated by giant tulip trees and white oak. Six acres surrounding the mouth of Donaldson Cave, reached by another trail, have also been designated a state nature preserve. The scene that meets your eye here—a small stream flowing from the cave's entrance and through a gorge whose slopes are thick with hardwood trees—is one of the loveliest in the state.

Park naturalists conduct walking tours into Donaldson Cave and also into Bronson Cave. At Twin Caves, you can take a short ride on an underground river while a naturalist tells you about the tiny blind cavefish swimming beneath you. To reach the park, go east on State Road 60 from Mitchell for about 3 miles; the park is on the north side of State Road 60; signs point the way. Spring Mill State Park, Box 68, Mitchell 47446; (812) 849–4081.

Spring Mill Inn is a combination of rustic charm and modern conveniences. Constructed in 1939 of native limestone and remodeled in 1976, the buff-colored building is located in the heart of the park. Guest rooms are decorated with colonial furniture, and the dining room serves three meals a day. Dinner usually features cornsticks made from meal ground in the park. Swimming is a year-round activity in the unique indoor-outdoor pool. Spring Mill Inn, Box 68, Mitchell 47446; (812) 849–4081.

Martin County

There's silver in them thar hills, if legend be truth! Since the first white man came to these parts, tales have abounded about the lost Indian treasure cave of McBride's Bluffs. For nearly 100 years, the Choctaw Indians lived in the bluffs area north of Shoals, taking shelter in one particular cave during severe weather. Absalom Shields, one of the first white settlers, told of the time when the Indians blindfolded him and took him to this cave, where he was shown a fabulous amount of silver crudely molded into bricks. Shortly after their disclosure to Shields, the Indians were forced to flee the area so hastily that they could not take the silver with them. They did, however, seal the entrance to the cave. Later, when one of their tribe was sent to claim the treasure, the trees he was to use as landmarks to guide him to the cave had been cleared away and he was never able to find the silver. Since then, a few isolated bars of silver have been found above ground, but the whereabouts of the cave remain a secret to this day. It's not for lack of trying, though—people still search for the silver.

The precipitous cliffs known as McBride's Bluffs, which soar 175 feet above the East Fork of the White River, are riddled with small caves. Because country roads may be unmarked, it's best to ask locally for exact directions to the bluffs, which lie approximately 5 miles north of Shoals and are shown on the official state highway map. Start out from Shoals going northwest on Highway 50/150, then turn north on State Road 450. Continue north to a side road about 1 1/2 miles north of Dover Village and turn east toward the White River; a single-lane gravel road winds along the riverbank at the base of the bluffs.

Martin County is one of the best places in the state for shun-piking (driving the back roads). Meandering country lanes lead past little-known havens of beauty—rugged hills, dense wood-lands, sheer sandstone cliffs—which are even more beautiful when wildflowers color the spring landscape and trees don their autumn hues.

Jug Rock, a striking sandstone monolith shaped like a bottle, is a product of centuries of erosion. Although it stretches to a height of 60 feet and is more than 15 feet in diameter, it is diffi-cult to see when the surrounding trees are heavy with foliage. It stands on the north side of Highway 50/150 a little to the north-west of Shoals, about a mile beyond the White River bridge, and is best seen from a small roadside pull-off on a high point along the highway. Look first for the large, flat slab that tops this unu-sual formation. (If, when traveling northwest from Shoals, you reach Highway 50/150's junction with State Road 450, you've gone too far.) You'll gain a better perspective of Jug Rock's dimen-sions if you descend the hillside to the forest floor.

Directly west of Shoals, you can see the bluffs of Beaver Bend, noted for the rare species of ferns that cling to the cliff and grow nearby. Beaver Bend is a sharp curve in the East Fork of the White River where Beaver Creek flows into it. These cliffs reach their loftiest height at Spout Spring, where water emerges from a pipe driven into the solid rock wall. The honeycombed cliff that overhangs the spring is layered with ochre and yellow rocks that soar 400 feet into the air. Again, ask for directions locally; an old country road passes near the base of the bluffs.

A few miles downriver from Beaver Bend, you can explore the picturesque Hindostan Falls area. In the early 1800s, the thriving community of Hindostan stood on the banks of the White River. It was abandoned in 1828, at the height of its prosperity, when a mysterious disease began killing its citizens. Only 6 feet high but nevertheless impressive, Hindostan Falls extends from one bank of the river to the other, creating scallops of white foam along the uneven path it follows. The power produced by the tremendous volume of water that passes over it each day was harnessed by the people of Hindostan to power their mills, while a large sand-stone ledge below the falls provided the rock for the mills' foun-dations. Still evident today are the large, square holes from which the rock was hewn, but the ledge is now used primarily by picnickers and fishermen looking for solitude. The pools below the falls teem with catfish, drum, crappie, white and smallmouth bass, buffalo, shad, and shuckers. Officially designated a state fishing area, the site also offers a free concrete boat launching ramp and some free primitive campsites. Do use caution here, though—the current is both strong and dangerous at times. To reach Hindostan Falls, go south from Shoals on Highway 50/150 to State Road 550, and turn west. The Falls area is on the south side of State Road 550. Open at all times; free. Contact the Regional Access Manager, Public Access South, RR 2, Box 140, Montgomery 47558; (812) 644-7731.

The Hoosier National Forest, just east of Hindostan Falls, occupies the southeast corner of Martin County. A drive along forest roads reveals a seemingly endless panorama of some of Nature's most stunning handiwork: huge rock bluffs, woods, waterfalls, streams, and box canyons.

Northeast of Shoals, boarding the north side of Highway 50, is Martin State Forest, one of the nicest surprises in the state forest system. Within its 6,132 acres, you can climb a fire tower, visit an arboretum or tour one of five demonstration areas to learn about forest management practices. The most spectacular hike in the forest takes you over a rugged, 3-mile trail that leads to Tank Spring, where water tumbles down 150 feet over moss-covered sandstone; come here in the spring when the greens are newborn and lustrous. Shady campsites atop a breezy ridge make this a great place to spend warm-weather days. Open at all times; free admission. Martin State Forest, P.O. Box K, Shoals 47581; (812) 247-3491.

The rolling hills of Martin County also spawned a Utopian dream. Called **Padanaram,** a name taken from the book of Genesis to signify a place of peace and rest, the commune began in 1966 with a five-room, 80-year-old farmhouse on 86 acres of land, five men, three women, two used pickup trucks, one mule and some donated farm equipment—not to mention a lot of faith and hard work. Today, it is a village of more than 250 people with a communal kitchen, bakery, school, nursery, auditorium and apartments; it is so successful that the sawmill, which provides its primary economic base, had to be moved 30 miles away to Bloomington where there was room for expansion. Padanaram now covers more than 1,500 acres of lakes, streams, woods, orchards, vineyards, and farm fields.

Daniel Wright, founder and chief spokesman for the commune, grew up in a commune near Des Moines, Iowa, and believes communal living offers the best type of existence possible. In 1972, NBC did a show on Padanaram, and the commentator called it the most viable of all the communes he had contacted. Visitors are welcome, although the villagers prefer that you come on a Sunday if possible, or attend the annual open house in mid-October. To reach Padanaram, go west from Bedford on State Road 158, through Silverville, toward the Crane Naval Ammunition Depot. Just before you reach Crane's entrance gate, you'll see a road veer off to the south. Follow this road to the village; a simple, rusted sign nailed to a tree will guide you along the way. Contact Padanaram Village, Route 1, Williams 47470; (812) 388-5571.

If you happen through Loogootee, you might want to stop in at Walker's Drug Company, 200 John F. Kennedy Ave. Quench your thirst at the soda fountain with a nickel Coke served in a 6-ounce glass. If you think you can handle it, go for the 10¢ or 15¢ size. This is nostalgia we can all appreciate.

Owner Fintan Walker and his wife Helen have learned by hearsay that only two other establishments in the United States still sell Coke for its original 1940s price. (A Coca Cola sales manager based in Evansville, Ind., says he doesn't know of *any* others.) To add to the pleasure, the Cokes are served in old-style Coke glasses, manufactured before the mid-60s. The old style reads "Drink Coca-Cola" rather than the "Enjoy Coca-Cola" of later years. Walker's, founded in the 1870s, has been in the same family for three generations. (812) 295-2094.

Monroe County

Indiana University, which sits in the heart of Bloomington, enrolls nearly 33,000 students from all over the world. The diverse cultures they represent have given rise to a cuisine that is international in scope and truly extraordinary for a town this size (52,000 people, sans students). Eateries specialize in Lebanese, Irish, French, Greek, Mexican, German, Italian, Ethiopian, and all styles of Chinese foods. Of course, American dishes and that staple of every college town in the country—pizza—are also available.

More than twenty pizza parlors thrive in Bloomington. One

serves a pizza chosen by *People* magazine as one of the top nine in the United States. You can try it for yourself at **Mother Bear's** [1428 East Third Street, (812) 332–4495] or just down the street at Bear's Place [1316 East Third Street, (812) 339–3460]. The former is your basic pizzeria, just for eating; the latter serves pizza only after 4:45 P.M., but offers big screen television, a classic movie series and live entertainment on the side. The sauce that brought Mother Bear's its fame is a bit on the spicy side, so arm yourself with lots of liquids.

If your tastebuds yearn for something continental, hasten to the Le Petit Cafe (308 West Sixth Street, (812) 334–9747), a small French restaurant that takes pride in its smallness. Chef Marina Ballor, who had never prepared a full meal before the cafe opened in 1977, has over the years developed her own style of cooking and several unique dishes (*Bon Appetit* magazine printed one of her recipes at a customer's request). The atmosphere is as different as the food—Marina's partner, Patrick Fiore, built the tables and adorned the walls with prints by French masters. Each day, the menu, which features only four or five entrees, is printed on a chalkboard. Good French cooking at reasonable prices; open 11:00 A.M. to 2:00 P.M. and 5:30 to 9:00 P.M. daily.

Located on the second floor at 430 East Kirkwood Street is The Wok, a family-owned restaurant that offers authentic dishes in all four styles of Chinese cooking. Food is prepared using traditional recipes from the Orient, rather than the Americanized versions to which most of us are accustomed, and chopsticks are provided. Weather permitting, you can dine on the outside terrace. Open for lunch and dinner, seven days a week; special buffets beginning at 11:00 A.M. on Saturday and Sunday. The Wok's authenticity was recently verified in a favorable review that appeared in *Ta Kung Pao,* the famous Hong Kong newspaper with a circulation of several million. (812) 339–4296.

Located in a quaint old home at 412 East Sixth Street is a small cafe/restaurant known as The Runcible Spoon, where patrons can sit upstairs, downstairs or outside in a Japanese garden. A 300-gallon aquarium occupies a dominant position on the main floor; more fish reside in a bathtub in the restroom. Jeff Danielson, the owner, likes to think that this relaxing atmosphere brings out the philosopher in everyone. The cuisine, ranging from Seoul barbecue to African ground nut soup to Indian mulligatawny, can only be described as eclectic. Coffee is freshly roasted, and the homemade bagels are an exclusive in Bloomington.

Open for three meals a day; 8:00 A.M. to 12:30 A.M. Monday through Thursday; 9:00 A.M. to 12:30 A.M. Friday and Saturday; 9:00 A.M. to 11:00 P.M. Sunday. The Runcible Spoon also serves a Sunday brunch. (812) 334–3997.

For gyros sandwiches unsurpassed anywhere, stop in at The Trojan Horse on the southeast corner of Kirkwood and Walnut streets. Paper-thin slices of beef and lamb are garnished with tomato slices, onion rings, and zaziki sauce, then served on pita bread. Have a Greek salad on the side and top it all off with a Greek pastry. Open 11:00 A.M. to 11:00 P.M. Monday through Thursday; 11:00 A.M. to midnight Friday and Saturday; 3:00 to 9:00 P.M. Sunday; (812) 332–1101.

Sometimes there's just no beating a plain old hamburger. Bloomingtonians-in-the-know brag about their Hinkle Burgers. Customers from California tell the Hinkle family they've heard of the burgers on the West Coast, and a nationwide radio survey a few years back named Hinkle's as one of eighty-two places in the United States where a truly "great hamburger" could be purchased. Hinkle's East is tucked in among a small complex of shops located on the southeast corner of Third and Jordan streets. It's open 10:30 A.M.–8 P.M. Monday through Friday; 11 A.M.–8 P.M. Saturday; and noon–8 P.M. Sunday; (812) 339–1311. Hinkle's West is at 206 South Adams St. Hours are 10 A.M.–6 P.M. Monday through Friday; 10 A.M.–4 P.M. Saturday; closed Sundays and holidays; (812) 339–3335.

Of course, Bloomington does boast a few pleasant activities that are not related to eating. One is a visit to the campus of Indiana University, noted for its magnificent trees. The IU Visitor Center, located next to the IU Foundation Building on State Road 46 By-Pass on the east side of the campus, can provide you with a free copy of *The Woodland Campus of Indiana University,* a guide to the natural woodland areas on campus that identifies more than 120 tree species. Contact the Indiana University Visitors Center (812) 855–6207.

Among the more unique attractions is the **Lilly Library of Rare Books and Manuscripts** (812–335–2452), which includes such treasures as a copy of the Gutenberg Bible, the first printing of the Declaration of Independence, one of the country's five major Lincoln collections, and one of two major Wadsworth collections. A recent exhibit displayed songwriter Hoagy Carmichael's original compositions. Although IU is renowned throughout the world for its School of Music, Hoagy obtained a law

127

degree here. One night in 1926, while sitting alone on a spooning wall at the edge of campus, thinking of two girls then in his life, he looked up at the starry sky and began whistling a tune. Unable to get the song off his mind, he dashed over to use the piano at a local hangout. A few minutes later, the proprietor closed up and tossed Hoagy out. Fortunately for the world, the song remained on his mind—it ultimately became *Stardust.*

If the campus looks familiar, it may be because you saw the award-winning movie, *Breaking Away.* It was filmed in Bloomington and featured the university's Little 500 Bicycle Race, held here each spring. The swimming hole in the movie was one of the water-filled limestone quarries you can see in the surrounding countryside.

Seven miles north of Bloomington on State Road 37, the Oliver Winery, Indiana's oldest and largest, offers a free tour and wine tasting. Owner Bill Oliver, a law professor at Indiana University, started his vineyards in 1971 and now produces 35,000 gallons of wine a year. Its best-known product, Camelot Mead, is a light and slightly sweet wine made from honey. If you're in the mood for lunch, you can have "a jug of wine, a loaf of bread" and your own "thou" beside you at a picnic table outside or at a table in the cozy tasting room inside. Cheeses, summer sausage, and crackers are also available. Open 11:00 A.M. to 6:00 P.M. Monday through Saturday, year-round; tours on Saturday or by appointment. Contact Oliver Wine Co., Inc., 8024 North Indiana 37, Bloomington 47401; (812) 876–5800.

Morgan-Monroe State Forest wanders over 23,916 acres, most of which occupy northeastern Monroe County. Nestled in a clearing in the midst of the woods is a rustic log cabin where a true get-away-from-it-all experience awaits you. Draper's Cabin is described by the state as primitive, and the description is apt. There's no electricity, all water has to be carried in, heat is provided by a stone fireplace, and you make your bed on the floor. The forest provides plenty of wood for the fireplace, but it's up to you to gather it and carry it in. Only dead material can be used, and no saws are allowed. You can cook in the fireplace or, if you bring your own grill, on a concrete slab outdoors. The cabin contains nary a stick of furniture, but two picnic tables are just outside the door. A few yards away, a small stream sometimes trickles by and sometimes doesn't–it depends on the rainfall.

Draper's Cabin, as it's known, is the only such cabin on any state-owned land, and you can rent the whole thing for $10.50 a night, including tax. The maximum stay is 14 days. Available by advance reservation from April to November through the Property Manager, Morgan-Monroe State Forest, 6220 Forest Rd., Martinsville 46151; or phone (317) 342–4026.

To reach the forest, go north from Bloomington on State Road 37 to Forest Road, the main entrance road, which runs east off of State Road 37 into the forest just before you reach the Morgan-Monroe county line. If you go in the spring or fall, you probably won't be able to resist a hike through the woods. Brochures for the trails, which include 9-mile and 7-mile loops and a ³/₄-mile pathway through the Scout Ridge State Nature Preserve, are available at the office building. If you do your walking during hunting season, it's best to wear bright colors.

Orange County

When Larry Bird first burst upon the professional basketball scene in 1979, he was promptly dubbed "the hick from French Lick" by many sportswriters across the nation. Since then, Larry Bird has established himself as the very heart of the Boston Celtics, and the sports world has learned two things—he sure can play basketball, and, shyness and Hoosier dialect aside, he is no hick. What's more, Bird's hometown of French Lick, although small, is also the home of the one of the most luxurious all-season resorts in the nation.

French Lick came into being because of some rich mineral springs that flowed from the hillsides. In 1837, to accommodate the hordes of people who flocked here to "take the waters," the French Lick Springs Hotel opened. Around the turn of the century, the hotel was purchased by Thomas Taggart, a nationally known political figure who served as mayor of Indianapolis and as U.S. Senator from Indiana. Taggart, who juggled his two careers, was named chairman of the National Democratic Party in 1904. His national prominence came at a time when spas were at the height of their popularity, and the elite of society and politics from all over the country descended upon French Lick to drink the waters from its spring and to partake of the mineral baths.

Gambling was added, luring even more visitors, including both celebrities and gangsters. In 1932, several state governors met here and decided to back Franklin Delano Roosevelt for president. The Vanderbilts, Morgans, and Whitneys came here to play, followed later by such stars as Roy Rogers, Dale Evans, and Gene Autry.

Today, the gambling is long since gone and the opulent era of the spas has drawn to a close, but the hotel, as lovely as ever with its tall white pillars, crystal chandeliers and plush carpeting, still operates as the French Lick Springs Resort. It stands in the midst of 2,600 acres of hills, woodlands, landscaped lawns and formal gardens, a gracious queen who has splendidly survived the test of time. Although the springs are still there, guests come today to relax in the peaceful setting and to enjoy a full range of activities—golf on two 18-hole courses, tennis on indoor or out-door courts, two swimming pools (one indoors for year-round use), skeet and trap shooting, horseback riding, bicycling and such games as bowling, shuffleboard, badminton, volleyball, horseshoes, and table tennis. There's even a modern-day version of the spa—a health and fitness center. From approximately De-cember to March, you can go skiing on six nearby slopes or skate on the hotel's ice rink.

As impressive as it all is, what you'll most likely remember as much as anything is the food. Such delights as New England codfish cakes, Spanish omelets, braised capon, South African lob-ster tail, peach Melba, strawberries Romanoff, and baked Alaska Vesuvius appear on the daily menu, along with favorite Hoosier foods.

Most facilities, many special activities, and transportation to and from French Lick Airport are included in the rates: Winter, $122, $117 or $127 per couple, per room, includes dinner and breakfast and some recreational facilities; April 16–June 10, $89, $84, $87 per person, dinner and breakfast and some recreational facilities; $157–$239 for a suite. There are also seasonal rates and many special package rates. Write French Lick Springs Resort, French Lick 47432; phone 1 (800) 457–4042.

About two miles up the road on State Road 56 is all that re-mains of the **West Baden Hotel**—an architectural masterpiece once known as the "most unique hotel on earth" and the "Carls-bad of America." It, too, flourished as a world-famous spa, but through the years it did not fare as well as French Lick's resort.

Begun in October, 1901, construction on the West Baden Hotel was completed 8 1/2 months later—an astonishing accomplish-ment in any day, but truly extraordinary given the technology of the time. Its imaginative owner, Col. Lee Sinclair, had conjured up visions of a sumptuous hotel that established architects of the day said was impossible to build. Urged on by his dauther Lillian, Colonel Sinclair finally found an enterprising young architect who accepted the challenge not only to build the hotel, but to do so for $414,000—with a $100-a-day penalty clause if construction took longer than the agreed-upon 200 working days.

When finished, the dome above the immense central atrium, larger than the dome at St. Peter's in Rome, was regarded as the "eighth wonder of the world"—200 feet in diameter, 130 feet above the floor, ribbed with 24 steel girders mounted on rollers to accommodate expansion and contraction. The atrium floor was covered with 12 million Italian marble tiles, and the elaborate sunken gardens were planted with rare flowers from Europe and the Orient. Circling the atrium and its gardens were 708 guest rooms on six floors.

West Baden Hotel thrived for thirty years, attracting an illustrious clientele that included the likes of Gen. John J. Pershing, J. M. Studebaker, and Diamond Jim Brady as well as the likes of Al Capone. In 1932, however, it became a casualty of the Great Depression.

Subsequently, it served as winter headquarters for the old Hagenbach-Wallace Circus, as a Jesuit school and as the home of Northwood Institute, a college that trains its students for employment in the hotel-restaurant field. During the Jesuits' tenancy, the face of the old hotel was altered forever. Some of the grander touches, they felt, were unseemly for their austere lifestyle. And so the Roman-style baths were wrecked and hauled away, the gardens were left untended, the lavish furniture was sold, the beautiful Moorish towers were removed from the roof, and the arabesque brickwork atop the building was straightened. The great dome, however, is still intact, and its effect upon visitors who enter the atrium is as powerful as ever. Now a registered National Historic Site, the building is being restored under new ownership for use once again as a hotel. Tour the atrium and grounds free of charge from 9:00 A.M. to 7:00 P.M. daily. For up-to-date information, contact the Springs Valley Chamber of Commerce, P.O. Box 347, French Lick, 47432; (812) 936–2405.

Railroad buffs will be intrigued by the Indiana Railway Museum, located just north of French Lick Springs Resort's parking lot on State Road 56. Operated as a nonprofit corporation, the museum has its headquarters in the Monon Railroad station. There you can board the French Lick, West Baden and Southern

Railway for a 1³/₄-hour, 20-mile round trip between French Lick and Cuzco, Ind. Old 97, a 1925 Baldwin steam locomotive, chugs away from the station and plunges into the wooded terrain of the Hoosier National Forest, offering its passengers views of rugged Orange County backcountry where no roads penetrate. Along the way, you'll pass through a 2,200-foot tunnel, one of Indiana's longest.

Although the museum intends for all its trips to be steam-powered, a diesel locomotive must sometimes be substituted. The museum currently has available six locomotives and 21 cars dating back to 1908. Trains depart each Saturday, Sunday, and holiday April through November.

The museum also operates a 2-mile round trip trolley ride between French Lick and West Baden, where you can disembark, tour the old hotel and its grounds at your leisure, and catch a ride back whenever you like. For additional information, write the Southern Railway Museum, Box 150, French Lick 47432; or phone (812) 936–2405.

Cuckoos, grandfathers and one-handed clocks tick away in the **House of Clocks Museum,** where you can learn about the history of clocks dating back to the early 1800s. The face of a fascinating mystery clock is imprinted with the question, "What Runs Me?" Eli Terry's Pillar and Scroll mantel clock, perfected in 1814, runs on wooden gears. Every hour, a chorus of clocks confides the time of day in a cacophony of voices. There are other antiques, too—a hand-carved Victorian bed, an eighteenth-century Empire sofa, chandeliers, candelabra, leather postal cards, an 1898 phonograph manufactured by Thomas Edison that plays cylindrical records, and an intriguing apple-peeler. You can explore the two-story museum at 225 College St., French Lick, which is open 9:00 A.M. to 5:00 P.M. Monday through Friday (closed Wednesday) and 1:00 to 4:00 P.M. Saturday, and Sunday; (812) 936–4238.

Kimball International manufactures pianos at its plant on State Road 56 in West Baden Springs, and visitors can watch master craftsmen assemble upright and grand pianos through all phases of the operation from stringing to final tuning. It's a unique experience that's free of charge, but make your arrangements at least two weeks in advance by writing Elvis Nelson, Box 432, French Lick 47432, or phoning (812) 936–4522. The tours are offered at 1:30 P.M. each working day to groups of ten or more, but you may be able to join an existing tour. If summer heat is a problem for you, you should know that the 300,000-square-foot plant has a concrete floor and no air conditioning.

Fern Davis, whose ancestors settled in this area in the late 1700s, knows both antiques and local history. She prides herself on the variety of pieces she offers at Fern's Antiques on the corner of Wells Street and Indiana Avenue in French Lick; (812) 936–9893.

No visit to Orange County would be complete without a stop at Punkin Center, 8 miles southeast of Orleans in the heart of the county's Amish country. The tiny hamlet is listed on the official state road map as Pumpkin Center, but don't you believe it. Add Gray says so, and since he's lived here all his life, he should know.

On Halloween Day in 1922, Add opened the **Punkin Center** General Store with $327.28 worth of groceries he'd purchased from a wholesaler in Orleans. He still has the receipt in his Museum of All Sorts of Stuff—a combination home, general store and barn presided over by Add and his charming wife, Mabel. Although the General Store is no longer open for business, it is still a repository for many of the Grays' relics and antiques. Swords, bells, plates (both dining and upper), saddles, sleighs, wagons, a crank-style telephone and the operator's switchboard, Colorado sagebrush, Indiana tickleweed, Spanish moss, Utah tumbleweed, a baby casket, an antique baseball uniform, an old-fashioned soda fountain, a roulette wheel, several scarecrows, a cast-iron chandelier from a Louisville, Ky., funeral home, a spring-operated churn, a collection of Indiana license plates that dates back to 1913 (including the only one ever made in the state with the number 1,000,000), a wooden Santa Claus suspended from the barn roof who waves his hand and jingles some sleigh bells at the flick of a switch—this list just skims the surface. Add, who claims he hasn't thrown anything away since 1917, has given new meaning to the words "pack rat."

When you arrive at Punkin Center, you might spot a sign that says "Come on in. We were expecting you. Everything else has gone wrong today." Ignore it. It's just Add's delightful sense of humor at work. Both Add and Mabel, who celebrated their fiftieth wedding anniversary in 1984, like nothing better than to welcome visitors and show them through their mindboggling accumulation of goods.

Sit and listen a spell as Add spins some yarns about folks like old Ma Hollis, who made wine and beer for the local farmers and occasionally took a few swigs herself. When Pa Hollis died suddenly, she said he fell and hit his head on the pine floor—but it was hickory bark they found in his forehead. Or Rough Tedrow, who could shinny up a tree and catch a coon bare-handed. During the Depression, he charged traveling salesmen 10¢ to watch him catch snapping turtles by the head. The biggest night in Punkin Center's history occurred in 1926, when Ray Trinkle dropped by the store carrying a lighted lantern and walked a mite too close to the gas tank. And many's the night the local folk stopped in to watch Bob McCoy spit on the store's pot-bellied stove from clear across the room. His accuracy was uncanny.

Across the road from Add and Mabel's home is Punkin Center's only other house. Add's brother Bert and his wife Evelyn live there, and although their collection can't begin to compare to Add's in size, they have antiques that, unlike Add's, are for sale.

The Punkin Center museum is open any time Add and Mabel are home. Take State Road 56 east from Paoli to a narrow, black-topped lane known as Potato Road (Add and other locals call it Tater Road). Take Potato Road north for about 2 miles, cross a bridge over Stamper Creek, and you'll be in Punkin Center. Follow these directions carefully, for there are two Punkin Centers shown on the Indiana map—the other one lies just a few miles to the east in adjoining Washington County. Add and Mabel would like to visit there someday, but to date they haven't had the time. The Grays' mailing address is RFD 1, Orleans 47452; (812) 723-2432.

Although the name Punkin Center conjures up pictures of Halloween, you might want to journey here in the spring and make a visit to Orleans at the same time. Orleans has been the official Dogwood Capital of Indiana since 1970, a few years after Mr. and Mrs. C. E. Wheeler started planting dogwood trees along State Road 37, one of the town's main thoroughfares. It was a labor of love for the Wheelers, who felt that the dogwood's pink and white blooms had no equal for beauty. Today, the trees cover a 12-mile stretch between Mitchell on the north and Paoli on the south, and more trees are added each year in what is now a community-wide project. They're usually in full bloom in late April and early May.

Orange County is also the site of two of the Hoosier State's most unusual natural landmarks. On the southern edge of Orangeville, which lies about 7 miles southwest of Orleans via county roads, you can view the Orangeville Rise of the Lost River.

An underground river surfaces here as an artesian spring, flowing from a cave into a 220-foot-wide rock-walled pit at the base of a limestone bluff. The three-acre preserve is well marked, and there's a pull-off for parking. For additional information, contact The Nature Conservancy, Indiana Field Office, 4200 North Michigan Rd., Indianapolis 46208; (317) 923–7547.

Not far from Paoli, on the edge of the Hoosier National Forest, is an eighty-acre tract of virgin woodland known as Pioneer Mothers Memorial Forest, whose magnificent trees are from 150 to 600 years old. Its crown jewel is the Walnut Cathedral, a moist cove that, according to the U.S. Department of the Interior, contains the finest black walnut trees of their kind in the entire country. From Paoli, go south on State Road 37 for about 1¼ miles to the Pioneer Mothers State Wayside on the east side of the road. From this picnic area, you can follow marked trails for a short distance into the Memorial Forest. Contact the Supervisor, Hoosier National Forest, 3527 Tenth St., Bedford 47421; (812) 275–5987.

Parke County

All of Parke County is a museum of covered bridges. Within its boundaries are more covered bridges than you'll find in any other county in the United States—more, in fact, than you'll find in most states. At last count, thirty-four of them remained intact. What's more, they're all authentic, with the two oldest dating back to 1856 and the youngster of the bunch to 1920. All 34 were placed on the National Register of Historical Sites in 1978.

Joe Sturm, a retired farmer and carpenter, has served as official bridge inspector for more than ten years and can relate all kinds of interesting facts about them. He can tell you, for instance, that so many bridges were built because of the numerous zigzagging streams in the county, that the only metal used in constructing them is in the bolts, and that the bridge at Mecca was built on dry ground and a nearby stream rerouted to pass under it.

Most of the bridges still support traffic, and the folks in Parke County have mapped out four automobile routes that provide access to most of them. A free map outlining each route is available at the Park County Tourist Information Center located in the old train depot on Highway 36 at the eastern edge of Rockville.

It's open 9:00 A.M. to 4:00 P.M. daily Memorial Day weekend to the first weekend of November, weekdays only the rest of the year; (317) 569–5226.

The northwest route leads you to West Union Bridge, at 315 feet the longest in the county. The community of Bridgeton, with its many unique shops, is a highlight of the southernmost route. Standing on the bank of Big Raccoon Creek, next to the double-span Bridgeton Bridge, is the Weise Mill. It's been grinding meal since it was built in 1823, making it the oldest-known grist mill west of the Allegheny Mountains that's still in service. Directly west of Rockville is the Sim Smith Bridge, which claims the distinction of being the county's only haunted bridge.

If you head northeast from Rockville, you'll come to Turkey Run State Park, noted for its steep ravines, sandstone formations and the Rocky Hollow-Falls Canyon State Nature Preserve that protects a lush primeval forest. The Narrows Bridge, one of the most photographed in the county, crosses Sugar Creek in the park. A tree-shaded inn in the park offers overnight accommodations in 52 rooms or 21 nearby cabins, two swimming pools, and four tennis courts. Write Turkey Run Inn, RR 1, Marshall 46859, or phone (317) 597–2211.

On Highway 41 north of Rockville, just before you reach the state park, stands the Gobbler's Knob Country Store, where you can purchase nostalgic wares that revive memories of grandmother—penny candies in jars, pickles from a barrel, sassafras bark, country hams, sunbonnets, corncob jelly, and carnival glass; (317) 597–2558.

Follow U.S. 36 east from Rockville for one mile and cross Billie Creek Bridge into a turn-of-the-century village and farmstead, where the crafts and skills of yesteryear are on vivid display. One of the finest living museums in the state, **Billie Creek Village** is open for nominal admission fee from noon to 5 P.M., Thursday through Sunday and holidays noon to 5 P.M. Memorial Day weekend through Labor Day weekend, and on several days in October. Write Billie Creek Village, RR 2, Box 27, Rockville 47872; phone (317) 569–3430.

Parke County originally had more than fifty covered bridges, but several were lost to fire, flood, and natural deterioration before a preservation effort was begun. Since 1957 the county has held a ten-day Covered Bridge Festival in October, a nationally recognized event that lures some 500,000 visitors.

Another popular festival is the late winter Maple Fair, which takes place when local sugar camps are producing maple syrup. For more information, write Parke County, Inc., P.O. Box 165, Rockville 47872; phone (317) 569–5226.

Perry County

Besides its bountiful natural beauty, this Ohio River county is worth visiting for its array of unusual monuments.

If Tell City has a trademark, it is the lifesize statue of William Tell and his son that serves as the centerpiece for the fountain in front of city hall. It is a reflection of the town's Swiss heritage and a tribute to the legendary Swiss hero from whom Tell City took its name. Town residents were delighted when, in 1974, plans were announced for the construction of the fountain that would honor the town's namesake, but they never dreamed it would cause such a fuss.

After the statue had been formed by Evansville sculptor Don Ingle, it was sent to a New York foundry to be cast in bronze. Ingle and his wife then personally picked up the 500-pound statue in New York, placed it in a rented U-Haul van and headed home for the formal dedication. Imagine their horror when, after spending the night in an Ohio motel, they discovered that the van—statue and all—had been stolen as they slept. Everyone got into the act, with local police and the FBI cooperating in a frantic search and news media throughout the country warning everyone to be on the lookout for the kidnapped William Tell. The nationwide furor was such that the thief eventually abandoned his ill-gotten gain on a side street in Cleveland, and the statue was escorted the rest of the way home without further ado. You can see him today in his place of honor atop the fountain—one arm holding his crossbow, the other arm around his son's shoulder, and not an apple in sight.

Poised above State Road 66 near Troy, a towering, 19-foot statue of Christ overlooks the Ohio River, arms extended in an eternal blessing of all who gaze upon it. It stands on a bluff once owned by Robert Fulton of steamboat fame and is now part of a summer camp for crippled children. Illuminated at night, the all-white statue is always visible to travelers on land or water.

At St. Augustine's Church in Leopold stands the Shrine of Our

Lady of Consolation, whose strange history dates back to the Civil War. Three young Union soldiers from Perry County, members of the church, were confined in the infamous prison at Andersonville, Georgia. They vowed to each other that if they lived through the horror of that experience they would donate a shrine to their church as a token of their gratitude. Miraculously, they all survived, and one of them personally made a trip to Belgium to oversee the making of an exact replica of a shrine he remembered seeing in a small village church there.

Some historians claim that, unable to obtain the replica he desired, the young man stole the original and transported it back to Indiana, sparking an international incident between the governments of the two countries. However, it happened that Leopold had been named for the Leopold who was then King of Belgium, who was so pleased to learn of his namesake that he allowed the shrine to remain there. It may be seen today, a statue of Mary and the infant Jesus, each wearing a white gown, a blue robe and a crown of jewels.

One of the Hoosier State's finest historical landmarks is now a vast and silent structure—the huge, castlelike cotton mill at Cannelton. From 1849 until 1965, the mill was a beehive of activity. Once the busiest industry in Indiana, it contained the most modern of textile machinery, rivaling the better-known mills of New England. Some 400 laborers operating 372 looms spun raw cotton into thread and cloth, and a good worker in the old days could sometimes earn as much as $4.50 a day. Union Army uniforms were made here during the Civil War.

Often honored for its architecture and described as one of the most outstanding engineering feats of its time in the Midwest, the mammoth stone structure is 60 feet wide by 280 feet long and has 5-foot-thick interior walls. Two copper-roofed towers, each more than 100 feet tall, serve as landmarks for Ohio River traffic. One of the towers held water that could be used to flood each of the five floors in case of fire, a constant threat in a cotton mill. The second tower, besides serving as a fire escape, was designed to reduce the risk of fire; it contained five trapdoors that were opened twice each working day so that air could be drawn down through a chimney to draw off accumulated lint.

It is a gaunt, gray ghost now, but still people come—to view the mill from the road, to marvel at its unusual style, to photograph a treasured relic of the past that has outlived its days of glory. Tours of the mill, located on Washington Street, may be arranged by phoning (812) 547–4247.

At the Steam Engine Museum on the Troesch farm near Adyeville you can have your picture taken in front of a moonshine still. Also sitting about are steam tractors and farm equipment, old fire trucks, a variety of bells, toys, and an old hearse. The museum is free, but for shoppers, there's an old barn full of antiques and hand-crafted items for sale. Follow the signs that lead you south from Adyeville for about ¾ of a mile. Open 8:00 A.M. to 5:00 P.M. on Thursday, Saturday and Sunday; (812) 357–5651.

For additional information about all these places, contact the Tell City Area Chamber of Commerce, P.O. Box 82, Tell City 47586; (812) 547–8286.

Back in Tell City, tour the **Tell City Pretzel Company,** which may be the only one in the United States and one of the few in the world that still produces pretzels the original way—by hand-twisting them. A Swiss baker brought the recipe with him from Europe when he settled here more than 100 years ago. Although the recipe is still a secret, passed down from owner to owner, visitors are welcome to watch the twisters at work each Monday through Friday from 7:00 A.M. until about 3:00 P.M. Phil Jamison, the current owner, and his family turn out about 8,000 pretzels a day. Pretzels are sold on the premises and by mail order. Write Tell City Pretzels, 532 Main Street, Tell City 47586; phone (812) 547–4631.

Pike County

The small town of Petersburg is home to 5,000 people, 17 churches and the only Atheist museum in the Western Hemisphere. On the front of the rustic building that houses the museum, owner Lloyd Thoren has placed the following message, a reflection of his beliefs: "If you cannot speak your mind, you are a slave."

What do you find in a museum for atheists? For one thing, a collection of books, magazines and pamphlets about the world's major religions—perhaps to point out the many conflicting viewpoints. Several murals depict the history of the earth and man, from the Big Bang to the DNA strand. Because Thoren feels that the development of transportation and of communication has been more important to the United States than religion, he has included his collection of vintage wheeled vehicles, ranging from a buggy to an electric citi-car.

"Basically," says Thoren, "ours is a cultural anthropological museum." He and his wife, Pam, are on hand to welcome you to what they describe as "the most ungodly place north of the Mason-Dixon line."

Generally open from 9:00 A.M. to 5:00 P.M. daily from late spring through early fall and at other times by appointment. Visitors traveling a long distance might want to contact the Thorens in advance to make sure the museum will be open when they arrive. A nominal admission fee is charged, but regular visitors and American Indians are admitted free.

To reach the museum from the center of Petersburg, go south on State Road 56/61 for about one mile. When you see a green highway sign reading "Pride's Creek Park," turn east onto the park road and follow it about 1/4 mile to the museum on the left. Contact the American Atheist Museum, RR 3, Box 55, Petersburg 47567; (812) 354–6608.

Posey County

In 1814, a group of German Lutheran separatists migrated westward from Pennsylvania to the verdant valley of the Wabash River. There they purchased some 30,000 acres of land along the riverbank and carved from the dense woodlands the personification of a dream—a tiny communal settlement they named Harmony. An industrious people, the Harmonists established a variety of successful industries that ranged from the making of fine silks to the distilling of whiskey, and their products were much in demand throughout the eastern United States. They developed prefabricated houses, dug tunnels beneath them, and used the cool air therein to air-condition their dwellings. Oranges were grown year-round in their greenhouses. Eventually, they found themselves with enough leisure time to start bickering among themselves, and in 1825 their leader, Father George Rapp, sold the entire town to Robert Owen, a wealthy industrialist from Scotland.

Owen envisioned a Utopia of a different sort, a commune that focused on innovative education and intellectual pursuits. His **New Harmony** lured scientists, artists, writers, and social reformers whose ideas and creations made a lasting impact on our country's history. America's first free public school system, kindergarten, day-care center, free library, trade school, woman's club, and civic dramatic club came to fruition here. One of Owen's sons became an eminent geologist and was commisioned to make the first survey of new government lands in the West. After that son was appointed U.S. Geologist in 1839, he ran the U.S. Geological Survey from New Harmony for 17 years. Another of Owen's sons entered Congress, became an early crusader for the rights of women, and drafted the legislation that established the Smithsonian Insitution. Yet another son became president of Indiana's Purdue University. Although many of the concepts developed at Owen's New Harmony have survived, the commune floundered in 1827. One reason for this was that its inhabitants did not possess the husbandry skills needed to feed its populace. While lofty ideas and ideals were being discussed inside, the hogs were invading the vegetables outside.

New Harmony was never deserted, however. Its reputation as an intellectual center gradually faded, but many residents stayed on, putting down roots that have kept the community alive to this day.

In the 1940s, Jane Owen, wife of a direct descendant of Robert Owen, visited here and was so entranced by what she saw that she initiated a restoration project. Today, people come from all over the country to take a 12-point tour that traces the history of New Harmony from its original log cabins to some striking structures added in recent years.

Enclosed within the brick walls of the Harmonist cemetery at the west end of Granary Street are more than 200 unmarked graves—symbolic of continued equality in death—and several Indian burial mounds. The Labyrinth, a fascinating maze of paths and hedges on the south edge of town, represents the twists and turns and choices that confront each of us in our passage through life.

Completed in 1979, the stark white Atheneum that rises from a meadow near the riverbank has garnered many honors for its architectural design. The Visitor's Center within periodically shows a film entitled "The New Harmony Experience" and exhibits a scale model of the original town.

Serving as the altar for the Roofless Church, a paved courtyard that's open to the sky, is a unique dome that's shaped like an inverted rosebud, but casts the shadow of a full-blown rose. Its design was inspired by writer George Sand, who remarked that the sky was the only roof vast enough to embrace all of worshipping humanity. When he visited here in 1963, Paul Tillich, the world-renowned philosopher and theologian, was so impressed by the Roofless Church that he said it alone justified our century. When Tillich died not long afterward, his ashes were buried in Tillich Park opposite the church.

One of the most beautiful sights at New Harmony, however, is a seasonal event orchestrated by Mother Nature. The first golden rain tree in the nation was planted at New Harmony, and today there is scarcely a lawn or street anywhere in town that does not boast at least one of these lovely trees. An ornamental tree that originated in the Orient, the golden rain tree is unusually beautiful throughout the year, but is most glorious around the third week in June when it bursts into full bloom, then sheds its petals in a virtual shower of brilliant gold. There's no place in the United States where this tree grows in greater quantity, and New Harmony celebrates its beauty each June with a festival.

Even the town's commercial district has a revitalized turn-of-the-century aura, And although it's not historic, the red brick **New Harmony Inn** is a charming mix of traditional and modern design that blends in well with its surroundings. Wood-burning fireplaces, rush-seated rockers, kitchenettes, living rooms and spiral staircases that lead to sleeping lofts are all available. Trees march right up to glass walls that enclose a heated pool, and the sky is always visible through a sliding glass roof. The beautifully landscaped grounds share the shoreline of a placid lake with open fields and patches of forest laced with biking and hiking paths. Rates vary seasonally. Contact the New Harmony Inn, New Harmony 47631; (812) 682–4491.

Next door, a gourmet restaurant, the Red Geranium, serves lunch and dinner six days a week. The spinach salad with house dressing, warm homemade bread, and Shaker lemon pie are really special. Dinners and children's menus are available. Hours are 11:00 A.M. to 11:00 P.M. Tuesday through Saturday, 11:00 A.M. to 8:00 P.M. Sunday; closed Mondays and some major holidays; (812) 682–4431.

New Harmony is easily explored on foot. Historic New Harmony, Inc. has its headquarters here and offers general information as well as guided tours for nominal fees; write them c/o Visitor Center, New Harmony 47631; or phone (812) 682–4474.

By driving south from New Harmony on State Road 69 for

about 24 miles, almost to the Ohio River, you are suddenly confronted with a scene that might have been transported here from the Deep South. **Hovey Lake** resembles a southern swamp, particularly in the slough areas to the east of the lake. Its waters are studded with huge bald cypress trees—one noteworthy old patriarch has lived to an approximate 240 years of age. Along the lakeshore are southern red oak, wild pecans, mistletoe, holly and swamp privet.

Birdwatchers spot great blue herons, American egrets, double-breasted cormorants and pileated woodpeckers. Osprey have been known to nest here, and white ibis, bald eagles, hawks, and owls frequent the area. In the autumn, usually beginning in the first week in October, some 500,000 ducks and geese arrive for the winter.

Hovey Lake, formed about 500 years ago, is an oxbow lake that occupies an old channel of the nearby Ohio River. It's now part of a 4,300-acre state fish and wildlife area, but even if you don't like to fish, you can rent a rowboat, glide among the majestic trees that rise from the surface of the water, and enjoy the serenity and seclusion of this lovely place. When seen through the mists of early morning, Hovey Lake takes on the aura of a dream.

Close to the launching ramp, you'll find an oak-shaded picnic area and forty-eight primitive campsites. Write Hovey Lake State Fish and Wildlife Area, RR 5, Mt. Vernon 47620; (812) 838–2927.

Putnam County

In the valley of Big Walnut Creek lies one of the most beautiful and unique natural areas in Indiana. The clear waters of the creek calmly meander southward through steep ravines studded with limestone outcroppings. A great blue heron rookery that has been continuously occupied for more than sixty years shares the forest with the great horned owl and more than 120 other species of birds. What is thought to be the largest living sugar maple in the world, as well as the two largest sassafras trees and the second biggest hemlock in Indiana, thrive within the preserve's confines. Located about 1 1/2 miles northeast of Bainbridge, the Big Walnut Valley Natural Area lies primarily along that part of the creek between the Pine Bluff Covered Bridge and the Rolling Stone Covered Bridge. It's open daily, free of charge, during daylight hours. For additional information and exact directions, contact The Nature Conservancy, Indiana Field Office, 4200 North Michigan Rd., Indianapolis 46208, (317) 923–7547; or the Green-castle Chamber of Commerce, P.O. Box 389, Greencastle 46135, (317) 653–4517.

Roachdale, a small village in the northern part of the county, is the site of one of the zaniest events held anywhere—an annual race for cockroaches. Each Fourth of July, contestants adorned with brightly-colored racing stripes line up in their appointed lanes atop a plywood course and await the official signal to start. Entrants with a tendency to wander at this critical time are kept in place with flypaper. At last, someone calls out, in true Indian-apolis 500 fashion, "Gentlemen and ladies! Start your cock-roaches!" and the race is on. The rules permit owners to place edible enticements behind the finish line, and that's usually all a cockroach with any get-up-and-go at all needs to spur him on his way.

The rules are simple—any trainer with a live roach may enter. And how, you might ask, do you train a roach? One gal claims she taught her bug to do isometrics.

It's not unusual to see racers from faraway states, but recently the contest went international. One lady hand-carried her roach—a thoroughbred—all the way from England. It didn't win, but they ran up a British flag in its honor.

If you have a roach that's into racing or if you'd just like some more information, write Jim Holland, Roachdale Lions Club, RR 1, Box 110, Roachdale 46172; (317) 596–4244.

Spencer County

Poised majestically atop a hill, the **St. Meinrad Benedictine Archabbey** emerges totally unexpectedly from the trees and hills of southeastern Spencer County. Your eyes are first drawn to the soaring twin spires of the Abbey Church, then to the entire complex of beautiful buildings that houses a theological school, college, monastery, and such income-producing enterprises as a publishing company, a winery, and a meat packing plant.

When the abbey was founded by immigrant missionaries from Switzerland in 1854, the monks themselves transported the sandstone from a quarry one mile distant, hand chipped it into the desired shape, and erected buildings patterned after the Euro-pean medieval style so vivid in their memories. Newer, more modern buildings appear among the old ones these days, but all interiors remain starkly simplistic in keeping with the order's dedication to a spiritual rather than materialistic lifestyle.

Visitors who roam the well-maintained grounds find themselves in the company of priests and brothers in simple black gowns, teachers, lay employees and some 400 students who are training for the priesthood. Although silence is part of the Benedictine life, it is expected only from 9:00 P.M. through breakfast the following day and at all times in the halls of the monastery. Otherwise, the monks and brothers are fun-loving, hospitable people who enjoy conversing with visitors. There's even a campus bar and pizzeria called The Unstable that's open two hours each weekday night and three hours on weekends.

You may join the monks for a worship service; Mass is performed in English. Brochures for self-guided tours may be picked up at the Guest House Office from 9:00 A.M. to 4:30 P.M. Monday through Saturday and 1:00 to 4:00 P.M. Sunday. Free guided tours are available by advance appointment; contact St. Meinrad Archabbey, St. Meinrad 47577; (812) 357–6611. The abbey is located on State Road 62, just south of Interstate 64, near the Perry-Spencer county line; follow the signs.

Two notable residents have made their homes in this county, and it would be tough to decide who is more famous—unless you are six years old or younger.

The U.S. Postal Service receives several million pieces of mail each Christmas addressed to Santa Claus, and it's all forwarded to Santa Claus's true domicile—a small town in southern Indiana. A few million more letters and packages are sent to the local postmaster with the request that they be stamped with the Santa Claus, Indiana, postmark before being sent on to their final destinations. Pretty heady stuff for a town with a population of about 500, give or take a few elves.

Although the town has borne its unusual name since 1852, it became world-famous only after Robert Ripley featured it in his "Believe It or Not" column in 1929. Such a hullabaloo followed that the annual Town Christmas Party had to be rescheduled for early October, when there was time to deal with such things. Today, the **Santa Claus Post Office,** whose stone front resembles a castle, probably gets more visitors than any other post office in the country. Folks just can't believe the stacks of mail they see there each year just before Christmas.

Elsewhere, there's a city park where a 22-foot statue of the jolly old man gazes down on the "little people of the world" to whom he is dedicated. Another Santa image sits atop a candy-striped water tower. The names of just about everything contribute to the aura of fantasy—Silver Bell Terrace, Donder Lane, Sled Run, Lake Rudolph, Lake Holly, Lake Noel, the Snowflake Drive-in, the Christmas Lake Village housing development, a newspaper called *Santa's Country.* Some town shops carry out the Christmas theme in their architecture, and Santa Claus Land opened in 1946 as the first theme park in the nation.

Recently, Santa Claus Land was renamed Holiday World, but it still has all the attractions that endeared it to countless children—and adults—in the past. Santa's headquarters are there, of course, and lots of toys, the animal farm where Santa's reindeer rest up for their arduous Christmas eve journey, a variety of live musical, magical and trained animal shows, and a bevy of rides. If you dismiss all this as child's play, you should see the buses full of senior citizens from all over that make regular visits here.

The one-price admission, extremely reasonable by today's standards, entitles a guest to ride all rides and see all shows and attractions; children two and under are admitted free. Hours may be expanded in the future, but at present Holiday World is open Memorial Day to Labor Day and weekends in April, May, September, October, 10:00 A.M. to dusk. Santa Claus, you see, must have some time for such trivial pursuits as preparing for Christmas. Write Holiday World, Box 36, Santa Claus 47579; (812) 937–4401. Santa Claus, the village, is located on State Road 245 in the north central part of the county.

Spencer County's second famous resident is immortalized in the pages of history books. When people think of Abraham Lincoln, they usually think of the states of Kentucky and Illinois, but it was in Indiana that a young Abe went to school, worked the land and grew to manhood. Abe's father, Thomas Lincoln, brought his small family here in 1816 and homesteaded 160 acres along the banks of Little Pigeon Creek. Indiana was a wilderness then, a forest of giant oaks, maples, and hickories where open views of even 200 yards were rare. Lincoln himself described it thus, in a poem he wrote many years after leaving the state:

"When first my father settled here
'Twas then the frontier line.
The panther's scream filled the night with fear,
And bears preyed on the swine."

In 1818, when Abe was nine and his sister Sarah was eleven, their beloved mother died, and little more than a year later, a lonely Thomas married Sara Bush Johnston. A widow with three children, she raised Abe and Sarah as though they were her own, lavishing them with such love and affection that she forever tarnished the image of the wicked stepmother. She recognized the intimations of future greatness in young Abe and encouraged him to study, and Abe, on his part, loved her as few children love even their natural parents. When an adult Abe said, "All that I am, or hope to be, I owe to my angel Mother," he was speaking of his stepmother.

Lincoln left Indiana when he was twenty-one and moved to Illinois with his family, but his tenure in Spencer County is honored in a series of memorials. The **Lincoln Boyhood National Memorial** is next door to Lincoln State Park on State Road 162, just south of Lincoln City. Abe's mother, Nancy Hanks Lincoln, is buried at the former, and her grave and the reconstructed Lincoln cabin may be visited in this 200-acre park. A living historical farm that covers eighty acres of the Lincolns' original homestead is worked as Abe and his father once worked it and provides a fascinating, accurate insight into a way of life that shaped one of our nation's greatest men.

At the handsome Visitor Center, you can view exhibits related to Lincoln's fourteen years in Indiana and see a twenty-seven minute film about his life. You can also learn much about the human side of Lincoln, little-known facts that breathe life into the saintly image. Young Abe, for instance, loved to wrestle and was recognized as one of the area's best tusslers. His great physical strength earned him the nickname of "young Hercules of Pigeon Creek," and he could hoist more weight and drive an ax deeper than any man around. In 1828, his horizons widened greatly when he accompanied the son of the richest man in the community on a flatboat journey down the Ohio and Mississippi rivers to New Orleans. And one can only speculate how the course of history might have differed if Abe had grown up in Kentucky where slavery was tolerated. The national memorial is open daily, year-round. Costumed interpreters work the farm from mid-April through September. Write Lincoln Boyhood National Memorial, National Park Service, Lincoln City 47552; (812) 937–4757.

The adjacent Lincoln State Park, which covers more than 1,800 acres, includes the grave of Lincoln's sister, who died in childbirth; the site of the Little Pigeon River Primitive Baptist Church where the Lincoln family worshipped; and the site of the first school attended by Abe, who was eleven years old at the time. You'll also find many opportunities here for outdoor recreation, as well as campsites and housekeeping cabins. Open daily, year-round, during daylight hours; nominal vehicle admission fee is charged from spring through fall. Write Lincoln State Park, Box 216, Lincoln City 47552; (812) 937–4710.

On the banks of the Ohio River just west of Troy, the Lincoln Ferry Landing State Wayside Park on State Road 66 preserves another historical segment of Abe's life. Here, as an employee of a local farmer, sixteen-year-old Abe operated a ferry across the mouth of Anderson Creek, a tributary of the Ohio now called Anderson River. To increase his income, Abe built himself a scow to carry passengers to Ohio River steamboats in midstream. His first experience with the legal profession came when he was hauled into a Kentucky court for ferrying passengers on the Ohio without a license (the Ohio River was considered part of Kentucky). Lincoln pleaded his own case, stating that he didn't believe the law applied to a ferryman who went only halfway across the river. Agreeing with him, the judge dismissed the case. Abe's fascination with the law began with that encounter.

Following State Road 66 west along the banks of the Ohio, you come to Rockport, where the Rockport Inn offers one of the most unusual lodging experiences in southern Indiana. This tiny hostelry, originally built as a private residence around 1855, contains just six bedrooms and four dining rooms. No two bedrooms are alike, but each has air conditioning and a private bath. Thoroughly renovated with painstaking care in recent years, the building retains as much of the original aura and design as the owners could achieve. Turn-of-the-century furnishings throughout contribute to the overall effect. Open year-round, the moderately-priced inn serves meals on a rotating basis. Breakfast and lunch are offered Monday through Friday and dinner Wednesday through Saturday. There's also a Saturday brunch, but no meals at all on Sunday. Write the Rockport Inn, Third at Walnut, Rockport 47635; (812) 649–2664.

Also in Rockport is the Lincoln Memorial Village. Although all 16 log cabins are reconstructions, they reflect the lifestyle of Lincoln's boyhood years, and you can learn more interesting facts about our 16th President here. Situated next to the Rockport City Park, the village is open daily 8:00 A.M. to 5:00 P.M. (812) 649–2242.

Vanderburgh County

Residents of Evansville have always known their city is tops; now the rest of the country knows it, too. In a recent study that rated the quality of life in 277 metropolitan areas across the nation, Evansville was the only Midwestern city to make the top ten.

Evansville came into being because of the Ohio River, and like most river towns, it has been exceedingly proud of that heritage. From May through October, the *Spirit of Evansville,* a sternwheeler riverboat, carries a maximum of 150 passengers on a variety of cruises up and down the Ohio River. Its turn-of-the-century decor and appointments offer a nostalgic journey into the past, but you can enjoy them as our ancestors never did—with air conditioning or heat as needed and modern restrooms.

On the one-hour afternoon cruises, your captain will point out landmarks along the way and share river tales and legends with you. One two-hour cruise offers dinner and dancing; the two-hour evening cruise, complete with moonlight and music, is pure romance.

If architecture is your cup of tea, you'll want to tour two esthetic treats in Evansville. The John Augustus Reitz Home at 224 S.E. First Street was erected in 1872 when Evansville was the hardwood capital of the country and Reitz was the "pioneer lumber king." Encircled by a black wrought-iron fence, the French Imperial house boasts three stories, seventeen rooms, ten fireplaces and a display of Victorian-era opulence in the parquet floors, gilded bronze chandeliers, stained glass windows, pier mirrors, gold leaf cornices, and rare carved woods. Some of the first-floor ceilings are canvas, handpainted in oil to match the original rugs. All heating units were turned on their sides and placed under the floor so that the radiators wouldn't show. The fireplaces were apparently for ornamentation only—they were never used. In the basement is a huge clothes dryer where clothes were hung on movable racks and dried by a gas heater beneath them.

The Reitz home sits in a seventeen-block historic district amid other massive homes built by wealthy owners who spent a considerable part of their fortunes trying to outdo the next fellow, but the home of the pioneer lumber king is the showplace of them all. Now a museum, it's open to the public from 1:00 to 4:00 P.M. Saturday and Sunday, May through November; and Wed. 1–4 P.M. during summer. Visitors are taken on a half-hour tour, with the

149

last tour beginning at 3:30 P.M. Nominal admission fee. Special tours may be arranged by calling (812) 423–3749.

The old courthouse that dominates the Evansville cityscape, built between 1888 and 1891, is one of the grandest in the country. During its construction, special excursion trains brought visitors from Louisville, St. Louis, and many other midwestern towns to admire what was then regarded as one of the most elegant buildings ever erected in the Midwest.

Its Indiana limestone face is encrusted with an unbelievable amount of sculptures and stone carvings, some of heroic proportions, each intricately detailed—fourteen statues, national emblems, ornamental friezes, cherubs, innumerable garlands of flora indigenous to the area, and Indiana's state seal. Inside, there are marble floors and wainscots, oak woodwork, brass handrails, silver-plated hardware, domes, and an awesome rotunda.

Abandoned by the county government in 1969, the old courthouse now houses boutiques, art galleries, import shops, clothing stores, and a community repertory company. You'll find the magnificent old building at the corner of Fourth and Vine. For a nominal fee, you can take a guided tour; (812) 423–3361.

At **Wesselman Park,** you'll find 210 acres of primeval woodland. A virgin forest is extremely rare, but this one is particularly unusual because it lies entirely within the limits of a city and is of such high quality (most stands of woodland in or near cities have been adversely affected by pollution). A melting pot of northern and southern botanical species, Wesselman Park Woods is dominated by sweet gum trees. Spring here is bright with the blossoms of dogwood and redbud trees and the wildflowers at their feet; autumn is a blaze of color. There's a nature center at the edge of the woods, where one-way glass provides a unique view of wildlife activity and a microphone brings sound and song indoors.

The woods, designated both a state nature preserve and a national natural landmark, make up approximately half of Wesselman Park; the remaining 200 acres offer typical recreational facilities, including a swimming pool. Along the park's northern boundary is a remnant stretch of the old Wabash and Erie Canal, the longest ever built in this country. Only two boats ever traveled its entire 468-mile length from Evansville to Toledo, Ohio.

The park lies on the east side of Evansville, just south of U.S. 460 (Morgan Ave.), at 551 North Boeke Road. Admission is free. The grounds are open daily, year-round, from early morning until sunset. The Nature Center is open summer: Tuesday through Saturday 8:30 A.M. to 5:00 P.M., Sunday noon to 5:00 P.M. Winter: Tuesday through Friday 8:30 A.M. to 4:30 P.M., Saturday 8:30 A.M. to 4:00 P.M., Sunday noon to 4:00 P.M. (812) 479-0771.

Moundbuilder Indians, too, found this part of the country to their liking. Sometime around A.D. 1300, they built a village on the banks of the Ohio River southeast of Evansville and stayed there for some 200 years before moving on. The eleven mounds they abandoned in this spot constitute the largest and best preserved group in the state. One, the central mound, covers more than four acres in area and measures 44 feet in height, making it one of the largest such structures in the eastern United States.

After years of archaeological excavations here, the 430-acre site was opened to the public as Angel Mounds State Historic Site. Visitors can view a simulated excavation site and many artifacts from the digs in a modern interpretive center, then walk the trails that lead among the mounds and reconstructed buildings of the Indian village. The memorial is located at 8215 Pollack Ave., 7 miles southeast of downtown Evansville. Free admission; open 9:00 A.M. to 5:00 P.M. Wednesday through Saturday; 1:00 to 5:00 P.M. Tuesday and Sunday; closed Mondays and major winter holidays; (812) 853-3956.

Evansville is a strong contender for the title of "Barbecue Capital of the Midwest," and several local restaurants work hard to support this claim. One satisfied customer who's apparently already voted for his favorite is Barry Goldwater. A glass case at Mac's Barbecue displays a personal letter from the U.S. Senator, in which Goldwater related that, even as he was writing, his wife was reheating some of Mac's barbecue in the kitchen, and it smelled delicious. Goldwater, as you probably know, hails from that hotbed of barbecue activity, the American Southwest.

Situated at 1409 East Maryland Street, Mac's is open from 10:30 A.M. to 9:00 P.M. Sunday through Thursday; 10:30 A.M. to 11:00 P.M. Friday and Saturday; (812) 425-1301.

Index

Index

Index